how to be better at . .

marketing

how to be better at . . .
marketing

Rod Davey
and
Anthony Jacks

**KOGAN
PAGE**

First published in 2000

Kogan Page Limited
120 Pentonville Road
London N1 9JN

© Touchstone Training and Consultancy, 2000

British Library Cataloguing in Publication Data

A CIP record for this book is available from the British Library.

ISBN 0 7494 3197 0

Typeset by JS Typesetting, Wellingborough, Northamptonshire
Printed and bound in Great Britain by Clays Ltd, St Ives plc

DEDICATION

For our friends at Witham Writers Group who prompted our meeting and brought this collaboration about.

CONTENTS

■ Contents ■

PREFACE

Making the business successful – and that means obtaining sufficient business to make a profit – is the most important thing an organization does. Nothing else – producing a unique product, ensuring exemplary quality, having the best people, or whatever – counts, if the level of revenue is not acting to secure the organization for the future. Most businesses seek not just to 'make a profit', but to meet carefully set financial targets that not only secure the short term (and pay the salaries), but also finance long-term success and growth. Even non-profit-making organizations that utilize marketing must be financially prudent.

Simplistically, marketing is the activity that has responsibility for 'bringing in the business'. In fact it does more than that. It plays a part in deciding what the business is, where it is going and certainly in identifying and securing customers and prompting them to buy and to go on buying. Marketing activity is often ill defined. It constitutes much more than the visible promotional and sales activity (important though that is) that it is often associated with, sometimes to the exclusion of other factors.

Marketing is not an option; it is a necessity. It is not simply a department, or a person. It is a whole way of going about conducting the business.

Real life

At the same time, marketing is not a routine. 'Doing marketing' is not sufficient to guarantee success, especially in these first years of a new millennium. We live in dynamic times. This is not simply a cliché – things really are changing as we watch. The information technology revolution is just one example. Managers are having to get to grips with new machinery and new methods, and the same technology is affecting all aspects of organizations' relationships with their customers, for example in terms of how communications work between them and how matters are handled – it is only comparatively recently, for instance, that you could have bought this book using e-commerce, through the likes of Amazon.com.

Change is not limited to things technical. It affects everything from products and services to competition and marketing methods. Marketing is essentially a creative process – as much art as science – and we must continually seek new ways of doing things to keep up with, or get ahead of, those who seek business from the same markets. Nothing can be taken for granted, and nothing stays the same. All the components of marketing, from pricing to promotion, must be constantly reviewed and fine-tuned to ensure they do the best possible job at any particular moment. This needs planning and a systematic approach, as well as flair and creativity.

The environment in which businesses operate is essentially hostile. Other people are not on your side, as it were, and many – both customers and competitors – will take advantage of any weakness in your business approach. The situation is not local, but international. Large companies regard the world as their market and, locally, competition is as likely to come from the other side of the world as from down the road. Nor is the situation temporary. Competitiveness is increasing, and this trend seems likely to continue, certainly in the foreseeable future. The only response to this should be an active one. Marketing must be professionally undertaken if it is to produce any chance of success. Nothing must be left to chance; no stone must be left unturned.

Making it work

Success in the market is dependent on a number of things: first, on a clear understanding of exactly what marketing is, how it works and how it can be utilized; and second, on going about it thoroughly in a way that matches the needs of the particular organization and reflects the realities of the marketplace in which it operates – not least in a way that relates accurately to customers, for marketing is, at base, customer-driven.

This book looks at both these aspects. It is intended to help whoever is responsible for marketing, and to demystify the process so that its constituent parts are laid bare. It dissects the various aspects of marketing, showing clearly the job each does and how it fits with and relates to the other aspects of the process, and indeed to other aspects of the business.

Above all, this book is intended to be action-orientated. Its role is to help you plan action and to make its implementation work. In showing how to be better at marketing, it lays out a plan for effective business development and thus, ultimately, for financial success.

Roderick Davey and Anthony Jacks
January 2000

THE MARKETING CHALLENGE

WHAT IS MARKETING?

Being better at marketing implies having a clear definition in mind, together with a precise understanding of what marketing is. As there is often so much confusion, both within industry and outside it, as to what marketing encompasses, it seems best to start by making clear what it is *not*.

It is not simply advertising or selling, although both are part of it. It is not actually any one thing at all. That it is ever thought so could be considered the fault of those with a vested interest in a particular facet of marketing, who emphasize that aspect over the others. It continues to be a somewhat nebulous concept. In practical terms, marketing can be defined in the following three ways:

❑ **a business philosophy**, that is seeing the business through the eyes of customers and ensuring profitability by providing them with value satisfaction;
❑ **a business function**, the total management function that co-ordinates the above approach, anticipating the demands of customers and identifying and satisfying their needs by providing the right products or services at the right time, place and price;
❑ **a series of techniques** that make the process possible and is involved in making it work, including advertising, market

research, sales, pricing and others ('marketing' is the umbrella term).

Any word with three somewhat differing definitions runs the risk of degenerating into a vague 'catch-all' term with no meaning at all. The official definition stated by the (UK) Chartered Institute of Marketing is: 'Marketing is the management process responsible for identifying, anticipating and satisfying customer requirement profitably'. Marketing guru Philip Kotler has defined it by stating: 'Marketing is the business function that identifies current unfulfilled needs and wants, defines and measures their magnitude, determines which target markets the organization can best serve, and decides on appropriate products, services, and programmes to serve these markets'. In a nutshell, marketing is industry's response to society's wants and needs.

Management guru Peter Drucker has defined it simply as: 'Marketing is looking at the business through the customer's eyes'. So if, after all your plans and calculations, you have not done this simple task, then you will be limiting your success.

THE BUSINESS FUNCTION

As stated above, marketing is the management function responsible for identifying, anticipating and satisfying customer requirements profitably. In any business, someone has to wear the marketing 'hat'. In larger firms, one person may head up a whole marketing department. In smaller companies, there may not be a marketing manager as such; the responsibilities may lie with the general manager, sales manager or whoever, or they may be shared amongst a number of people. Whoever is involved and however it is arranged, the final responsibility must be clear, and sufficient time must be found to fulfil all the necessary marketing functions. Perhaps, by definition, the person with marketing responsibilities should be a good delegator! Whoever it is, in a very real way, is in charge of the company's future.

THE TECHNIQUES EMPLOYED

The techniques include not just selling and advertising but all things concerned with implementing marketing in all its aspects. These include market research, product development, pricing, and all the presentational and promotional techniques such as selling, merchandising, direct mail, public relations, sales promotions, advertising, telesales, etc. All are touched on as we progress through the book.

THE ONGOING PROCESS

The marketing process is designed to 'bring in the business' by utilizing and deploying the various techniques on a continuous basis, and doing so appropriately and creatively to make success more certain. Marketing is not a 'profit panacea'. It cannot guarantee success by itself, nor can it be applied 'by rote' – the skill of those in marketing lies in precisely *how* they act in an area that is sometimes referred to, rightly, as being as much an art as a science.

Everyone in a profit-making organization, whether they like it or not, is involved in selling the company and its product. It starts with matters as straightforward as reception: the people who answer the phone (who should 'speak with a smile in their voice'), the time they take to do so and the impression they create are all, in fact, part of marketing. This is often the customer's first contact with a business and it indicates how professional that business is. Other elements add to the image: how quick delivery is, and how problems are dealt with (all organizations have problems, however good they are). All these factors have a bearing on whether people will want to deal with the company. Marketing exists in a permanently vulnerable state; literally one rude, ill-thought-out comment can destroy years of hard work. All the 'minor things' are worth keeping a careful eye on to ensure they work and contribute positively.

This idea of the sensitivity of marketing is a theme to which we will return. Small differences in many activities can change results – for better or worse – significantly.

The company function

Every company has three basic functions that must interact effectively. Large organizations can suffer from 'empire building', and 'them against us' situations can arise in any organization. One group can pursue its own objectives in a vacuum, rather as if other parts of the organization did not exist. Any lack of co-ordination can be divisive and should be discouraged if all is to work well.

The three basic functions are:

❑ finance;
❑ production;
❑ marketing.

There are also two major resources:

❑ capital (money);
❑ labour (human resources).

Each function has different tasks and different objectives – often each focuses on a different time-scale, attracts different types of people, and regards money in a different way. Despite the fact that all contribute towards the same company objectives (or should do so), there is inevitably internal conflict between, say, marketing and production (the amount of product it is thought should be produced and what may be sold), or between production and finance. (Organizations vary. 'Production' usually implies factories and tangible products, but everything has to be produced. For example, software is not in the same category as, say, a motor car, but has to be produced just the same. The team of people who audit your company's accounts represent the production side of their accountancy firm. Both products and services are involved here.)

If there is a certain amount of internal friction in your company, then relax: this is normal. You cannot really expect many disparate people, all with their own 'local' objectives and priorities, automatically to agree on everything, though ensuring all work effectively in a co-ordinated way is a major factor in ensuring success.

Marketing, and promotional activity in particular, represents an important means of affecting customer choice – you can actively put forward those messages you feel will signal the nature, quality and desirability of your products or services. If customers see quality signalled in the promotion, they may surmise that these standards of quality are consistent throughout the firm. Some companies major on the quality aspect of what they do, albeit in different ways (in the car market, for instance, BMW highlights engineering excellence, Volkswagen reliability).

To market intelligently, you must be able to see yourself from the customer's point of view. Part of taking up the customer's perspective is being able to think in terms of benefits rather than services. A customer is not looking just for the 'product', whatever it is, but for the benefits purchasing it will bring; for example, people do not buy an electric drill because they want an electric drill for itself, but because there is a need to make holes. The 'benefit' derived from the drill is the holes it makes, and thus ultimately its ability to help put up shelves or whatever (and thus create extra storage space and reduce clutter, which may be the primary need in customer terms).

Whatever the specific technical nature of what is being provided, customers are looking for assistance in solving problems. Whether this involves, say, buying a holiday to give them a rest after a busy work period or selecting a destination that will impress the neighbours (or both), the choice made will be to achieve *their* ends. However, in many fields, for instance with many technical products, if you can move the customers' perception away from regarding you as a mere supplier of goods or services, and into being seen in an advisory capacity, then you can build a special relationship that will set you apart from your competition.

Another example reinforces this last point: a company seeking a creative graphic design input, for instance, does not simply want a smart new brochure; it wants more business, or to achieve the successful introduction of a new product. The brochure is a means to an end, and the design is a step further back still. The benefits will ultimately be seen in the improvement of profitability. Benefits are what customers want your product or service to *do* for them. It is important, therefore, to be able to identify the particular benefits that will interest a given customer.

MAKING MARKETING WORK

Appropriate marketing action needs to be based on a wide appreciation and analysis of the needs of the business and the situation in the market. Marketing activity cannot, or rather must not, be ad hoc, with a little being fitted in as and when time allows. Marketing must be constantly reassessed to ensure it is performing at its best, because even the best performance can be improved, and because situations constantly change. Making marketing better must be an ever-present preoccupation.

Review of the process starts with the planning stage. Every business needs a plan, and a key element of such a plan is the marketing plan. Chapter 2 looks at investigating the market. Chapter 3 then looks at the planning process, and Chapter 4 at the concept of product positioning and pricing. With everything organized, consideration needs to be given to how to get what is sold to market, and Chapter 5 looks at the process of distribution and how it contributes to making marketing successful. Promotional activity, covering everything from what letterhead the firm has to advertising and public relations, and how it is planned and co-ordinated, is the subject of Chapter 6. The role of personal selling, and customer care and service, are investigated in chapters 7 and 8.

Chapters 9, 10 and 11 look at dealing with planning and managing marketing at the level of individual customers, at the need to incorporate the changing world of information technology

(IT) and to make it work for us and, last, at keeping control of everything that is done.

Throughout the review, the old adage, 'Marketing is too important to leave to marketing people', should be kept in mind – you must carry everyone with you if your endeavours are to result in success. Any organization is only as strong as the weakest link in the chain. Involving people makes marketing better, almost by definition.

Marketing is an essentially *creative* process, which has some scientific basis, but no absolute guarantee of success. Effective marketing reduces the risk of failure, or rather – let us be positive – increases the chances of success. One constant is that customers will be increasingly demanding, fickle and unpredictable and therefore marketing, however effective, always carries an element of risk. On the other hand, it is an exciting aspect of any business – and a vital one. When it goes well, it produces considerable satisfaction, and it is at such times that marketing people tend to become convinced that the success is *all* down to marketing, despite the fact that a wider range of influences is always at work.

Marketing is much more than simply a department, or a body of techniques; it is central to the whole reason for an organization's existence and its relationship with its market and customers. While many of a company's activities are important, it is true to say that profits can only be created externally: profit comes from the market. To pick up on the title of this chapter, the marketing challenge is to create a situation where customers buy in sufficient quantity, thereby producing the right revenue at the right time, as otherwise the business operation will not be commercially viable. Marketing has to produce convincing reasons for customers to buy, which are more powerful than those relating to competitors' products. Whatever the many elements involved, the key is to focus on customer needs and to set out to satisfy them at a profit, because without profit there is no business.

2

INVESTIGATING THE MARKET

Whatever you sell, it needs a market. A market consists of consumers, actual or potential, and all are individuals. To communicate with as many as is necessary, it makes sense to think of them as comprising discrete groups ('segments'). This way of thinking facilitates a whole range of ways of ensuring that marketing effort is effective. It is helpful, first, to define the concept.

THE CONCEPT OF MARKET SEGMENTATION

When you sell something, many people may buy it (the market), but not all will do so for the same reason or use. Any market can be broken down into smaller markets or segments, and ultimately the segments can be broken down into niche markets (a niche is simply the smallest manifestation of the segmentation idea). Niche markets can be very profitable, and represent the final level of customer identification. If you have identified all your markets, and your market knowledge of them is considerable, then all things being equal you have the foundation for effective marketing. The motor industry makes a good example to illustrate segmentation in action. People in general buy cars for reasons that include status, carrying capacity, economy, and more; but the division can also be specific: for instance, a specific individual buys (say) a family-sized car with economy and status in mind. A car that is more economical, yet seen as undistinguished, may not appeal (think of the persistently low image of diesel cars).

People who are in one segment will not necessarily move to another. This leads to the definition of a segment as: a group of actual and potential customers with the same needs, which similar products can therefore satisfy.

Even in what are perceived as 'mass markets', like soap or soup, customers buy for different reasons and uses. If these different uses can be identified, then 'cherry picking' or market specialization can occur, giving rise to extra profit. However, not all market segments work well alongside each other – would a Porsche pick-up truck have the same appeal as their sports cars? – and therefore many companies specialize, focusing their efforts on fewer than the total number of segments available. Analysis shows that even for products such as industrial equipment and components, and for services such as accountancy and hotels, market segmentation exists. So how big must a segment, or niche for that matter, actually be? Well, the group has to be of sufficient size to define, and to make a separate tailored marketing approach worth while. Ultimately it is a question of cost and return rather than solely numbers of people.

Classically, a segment must:

❏ be homogeneous;
❏ constitute a group large enough to exploit;
❏ have potential that can be quantified and qualified;
❏ be accessible within a given cost–time frame.

Even when a clear segment has been identified, it does not mean a product marketed to that sector will be guaranteed success for evermore. Products and services are not eternal.

PRODUCT LIFE-CYCLE

Products do not last for ever. Technology is always improving and fashions and opinions changing, so products have a life span. Some are ephemeral like newspapers and pop records. Others were ubiquitous even to our grandparents: consider HP Sauce,

Coca-Cola, Persil, or Bovril. Some fade away when they have reached the end of their life-cycle; others may be destroyed by technology. Look at the way the fax machine destroyed the market for telex machines and, in the 50s, transistors did the same for valve radios. How long will there be a significant market for fax machines now so many people have come to prefer e-mail? Some products can be destroyed by legislation, as were asbestos brake shoes, ousted when asbestos was outlawed on health grounds. Some can enjoy a revival of interest, like classic cars. This is what makes the marketplace so interesting; marketing is only restricted by lack of imagination and good ideas.

For most products the sine wave in Figure 2.1 is typical. Similar graphs may have a steeper start where the product is inexpensive relative to earnings, or novel – or both – achieving universal acclaim and high sales overnight, as with the introduction of the Rubik's cube or, more recently, the Harry Potter books. Some may have a vertical fall-off, like the asbestos brake shoes, but most follow a similar pattern to the graph shown, with variations only in the overall time-scale. If you doubt such life-cycles exist, you need look no further than a cookery or motor magazine of 50 years ago to see how many products featured have disappeared.

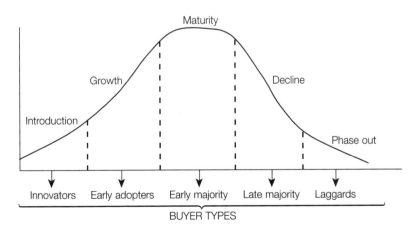

Figure 2.1 Product life-cycle

In recent years, the level of failure of new products launched is nine out of ten – most hardly embark on their life-cycle but are snuffed out in early childhood, so to speak.

Introduction: The product may start slowly, dependent on price and demand, and may require significant investment to get it going.
Growth: Market knowledge and purchase speed up, profitability grows, and long-term plans are made for the product.
Maturity: Sales growth slows down, but this is likely to be the product's most profitable time. Work will be required to keep the product at this stage, and there is always the threat of decline ahead.
Decline: This is inevitable. Legislation may kill it, as with asbestos products. Although with most goods there is a decline in revenue, with skilful marketing the curve can be more shallow and, with all fixed costs paid, good profit can be extended.
Phase out: The product dies or is revamped into something else. The cost to continue may outweigh the profit.

You can see from the explanation above how a product evolves. Sometimes products are ahead of their time and need time to gain acceptance. For example, even the motor car took time to become established.

Marketing can help the product gain acceptance. In all cases it has specific goals. It must aim to:

❏ speed the growth phase;
❏ extend the period of maturity;
❏ slow decline.

Such strategies will maximize revenue and profit. A number of changes, significant in their own right, may ultimately lead to even more radical development. Motor cars, for example, gave us spark plugs, dynamos, electric starters and more.

With a clear view of markets and how products can perform in them, the next job is actively to investigate the details of target markets. It is said that information is power, and in marketing it can make the difference between profit and loss. The prime form of such investigation is research.

THE NEED TO RESEARCH THE MARKET

The two basic purposes of research are:

❏ To reduce uncertainty when plans are being made, whether these relate to the whole marketing operation or to components of the marketing mix such as advertising or sales promotion (remember that, as was said, nine out of ten new products fail);
❏ To monitor performance after the plans have been put into operation. Monitoring has two functions: it helps control the execution of the company's operational plan, and it makes a contribution to long-term strategic planning.

Types and purposes of research

In essence research covers all the *finding out* activities of marketing. There are five major types:

1. *Market research*: Investigates the market, ie who buys what, in what quantity and where.
2. *Product research*: Reviews what customers feel is right or wrong with the products of the company, or of its competitors.
3. *Marketing method research*: Asks whether the methods used are working and whether customers like them; for instance, it looks at whether the company is communicating and distributing effectively.
4. *Motivational research*: Examines why people buy the products they do and how they feel about them.
5. *Attitude surveys*: Ask what customers' attitudes are to products and the companies that make those products.

HOW RESEARCH AFFECTS MARKETING ACTIVITY

The focus of research is historical: it can only investigate the past. This can be very helpful in *predicting* future behaviour, but it cannot guarantee it. When attempts are made (for example, with opinion polls or intention surveys), then serious errors can be made and less than 100 per cent accuracy is to be expected. The role of research is to improve the factual basis upon which forecasts and decisions are made, and thus reduce risk. The difference between researching the past and predicting the future must be clearly recognized.

The very first question that needs to be asked is *why* research is being done. This might appear a stupid question, but if the research is being done as a knee-jerk reaction to directives, with no intention of using and implementing the findings, then someone must have the courage to tell the company to save its money. Many blue-chip companies have spent many thousands of pounds on good analysis, only to ignore the results and implement nothing. Research undertaken must instigate change, even if only to the way the company sees itself in the marketplace. So whatever you can use to give yourself and your company a marketing edge must make both your position within the company and your company's position within the market just that little bit safer.

The idea of research links to the whole of marketing planning, where one all-embracing technique deserves a mention.

SWOTs

No book on marketing would be complete without mentioning 'SWOTs', the acronym for 'strengths and weaknesses, opportunities and threats', S and W being used inside the company and O and T outside. Together SWOTs provide a systematic way of analysing marketing activity. What is done may be formal and extensive, but the concept provides a practical basis for a brief yet thorough and objective look at how things stand. Even at its simplest it can be useful, and the omission of this sort of thinking is dangerous. Some examples of the points it might identify:

Strengths	Quality base product
	Dedicated transport service
Weaknesses	Lack of ISO 9000
	Not capitalizing on industrial business
Opportunities	Building long-term commitment from customers
	Provide tailored packages and services
Threats	Locally based competitors
	New products planned by competition

This kind of analysis is vital to marketing and, provided it is used sensibly and sensitively, can be useful not only for the information itself, but also in the conveying of information around the organization. It need not be just an analysis of the business as a whole, but can also be used from a subjective point of view by whoever undertakes the review. One possible danger is that the process may deteriorate into a form of introspective analysis, or may become analysis for analysis' sake. It is important that all the specifics of your particular type of operation are covered, as the nature of business can be very diverse. It is a very simple approach, which can be used effectively to canvass all the best ideas, if everyone on the team is allowed to contribute.

THE USE OF MARKET RESEARCH

The information you seek may cover many disparate things or it may be in just one narrow field. Whatever you seek should define opportunities for product development and/or market strategy. Market research can show whether marketing strategies are well targeted, and identify market opportunities or changes that are required by customers. It may tend to confirm issues that are already well known in a market but, if well planned and effective, will also, depending on the questions asked, identify new opportunities, market niches or ways to improve sales or communications. It can cover markets both present and future, and should reduce uncertainty in decision-making, monitor the effects of decisions taken and identify the performance of a company or product in the market.

Here are some examples of key uses for market research. They are by no means exhaustive, and you will need to define your own, depending on your requirements:

❏ to identify the size, shape and nature of a market, in order to understand it and its opportunities;
❏ to obtain information to help understand who the customers are, and the way in which they buy and use certain products;
❏ to evaluate customer service, assessing what customers feel about the services they receive;
❏ to investigate the strengths and weaknesses of your and competitors' products, and the level of trade and customer support the company enjoys;
❏ to test product ideas and strategies as a help in defining their most effective use;
❏ to monitor the effectiveness of strategies;
❏ to achieve better targeting as a result of understanding how advertising influences consumer choice;
❏ to help define when marketing expenditure, promotions and targeting need to be adjusted or improved;
❏ to identify changes in the market that will affect how marketing proceeds in the future.

Market research is not just a first check after action has been taken, but is useful ahead of any action. It is also useful if refinements and changes can be made even as operations proceed. Most companies are concerned whether the exercise is a worthwhile investment, especially when there are tight budgets. The best results come when marketing and sales planning is influenced by research information. Even threats in the marketplace can be a marketing opportunity. A discovery that consumers favour a development being made by a competitor might lead to defensive action that develops into a whole new initiative.

The next question is: what research is required? This is a fundamental question, and time needs to be taken to get the answer right. Together with how any research is to be done, it is vital – the wrong decision can lead not to useful information, but to an expensive pile of useless paper. Every detail is important, for example making sure with any questionnaires that there are no ambiguities, and that the respondent is not led to draw the wrong conclusion by inappropriate questions being placed together.

A traditionally stated definition of market research is: 'The systematic problem analysis, model-building and fact-finding for the purpose of improved decision-making and control in the marketing of goods and services'.

This implies that research is not just an information tool, but a means of providing guidance to help improve the abilities of management as well as helping management control the marketing mix. It can be used to help decide on the marketing strategy required to meet the challenge of new opportunities and which of these to approach now, as well as the key areas of interest for the future.

INFORMATION SOURCES

So what information is available and where can it be obtained? A wide variety of sources exist, as do ways of accessing them. Key methods, which illustrate the range of possibilities, are described below:

❑ Identifying existing information is called 'desk research'. This can be very simple, for example a local library has various magazines and newspapers, together with various trade directories and all sorts of company information. There are also specific trade journals, which your company may take on a routine basis. Yellow Pages and the Thomson guide are also useful but, as this is general information that you can presume competitors may also be using, why not try a more modern approach and utilize the World Wide Web? There are lists of companies available in floppy disk or CD-ROM form, which you can purchase from magazines, but you should first make sure that the information is in a form useful to you, and that it is up to date. You can also use specialist information-compiling agencies and online databases.

❑ Simple 'home-grown' research can also produce valuable information. For example, the surveys taken of hotel or restaurant users through short questionnaires completed in their bedrooms or at restaurant tables can mount up over time and paint a useful picture.

❑ Using other specific systems can help your business. For instance, an enormous amount of information is collected by retailers about shopping habits (nowadays largely through more and more sophisticated electronic cash point equipment), and this may be made available (sold!) to others.

❑ A fully fledged market survey is designed to do just what you want.

When you undertake fresh research, you should consider the research methodology to use.

Techniques of research

Two key factors in research are:

❑ *Sampling*: The commonest sampling methods are random and quota. The latter is cheaper to implement, as you choose by classification, for example people over 65; you screen out what you do not need. Sampling uses probability theory to predict the characteristics of a large number from a small section within defined limits.

❑ *Questionnaires*: These must be carefully designed to ensure the forming of the questions does not bias the answer. Questionnaires can be conducted in person, on the telephone, or by post. There is an inverse correlation between accuracy and cost. In some types of research, eg motivational studies on cars, group interviews are often used.

RUNNING THE RESEARCH PROJECT

Management must first decide as accurately as possible what it needs to know. Asking for 'all about something' is usually impractical, expensive, and could end up producing an unwieldy amount of data. For the exercise to be worth while, it will need to answer the following questions:

❑ What decisions do we have to make?
❑ About what?
❑ Where do we get the information?
❑ How accurate does it need to be?
❑ How quickly do we need it and why?

Another consideration is who is to run the research. Should it be done in-house with the problem of possible bias, or via external specialists who would be objective but might cost more? Usually the sales staff will be too busy (if not, why not?) and few firms these days have spare personnel, so an agency may be essential and, at the end of the day, cost-effective.

All aspects of the project must be clearly defined, and acceptable timings and tolerances set. Several proposals should be sought if outside agents are to be used, to ensure the best approach is selected. After the research is completed, the results should be checked against other data if possible, to confirm the findings. Decisions can then be made on the facts obtained, and a programme of action implemented. If no decisions are taken on the results, then it may as well be just another document for the shredder.

Well-directed research is almost always useful, even that based on something simple such as the collective experience of company staff. However, bigger decisions need a bigger budget, as you need more facts; and if you employ a specialist you will at least always have someone to blame if it goes wrong! Let us presume that you have done the research before the research well, so you can win in three ways:

1. It will confirm management's ideas and experiences that it is making the right decisions.
2. The research can provide new information about unknown aspects that give a new focus to the business.
3. The research material may prove a starting point, and prompt further, more relevant or detailed research programmes for the future.

EVALUATION OF RESULTS

So now you have before you the body of evidence you will use to influence the future. You may be a large international company and have used everything at your disposal: internal records, published information and field surveys; alternatively, you may be a small family firm just using published information, objective views and simple customer checks. Whatever analysis tools you use, each should be looked at on its own first, before all the information is brought together. This will act as an independent control and, to some degree, back up the other data, which may stop the reinforcement of existing prejudices towards the market. It must be remembered that this information is the historical basis for defining the future, so it will not be complete.

Research cannot make decisions for you. Do not rule out the considerable judgement and experience that may exist within your firm: they are a vital part of any research undertaken. They must play their part in deciding what action needs to follow. Whatever the brief, whether it is broad in nature covering all your products, or concentrating on just one market segment, the information compiled must be sound. Research is a means to an end; it must have the ability to deliver.

Marketing is always better when conducted in the full glare of knowledge.

3

CREATING A PLAN

THE PRINCIPLES OF MARKET PLANNING

Now you have the embryo of an idea that you have researched fully, you need to develop it into a plan of how to take that idea forward. This needs a logical and chronologically sequential approach, and your thinking must always allow for the unexpected. In this chapter, we highlight some of the key issues, commend the process and show how it can act as a foundation for making marketing work and for making it better over time.

The idea is that, with the planned application of sound marketing principles, the market plan will be simple, and all the rest will come as if by magic. However, the biggest, best and most assured of companies can make the most almighty mess of things. Planning may not be a panacea, but it is necessary. By analysing what you want to achieve, how far you are towards your goal, and what action you will take to implement the plan, you will have a firm basis for action.

Most management and marketing people have their pet saying recommending planning. Such sayings are simple and sensible premises, which companies and marketers ignore at their peril. 'Plan the work and work the plan' is one such pithy *bon mot*, which is well worth remembering. It all starts with having a clear view of all the aspects of your business. A taxi company may limit itself to taking customers by car around town. A more entrepreneurial one will go further afield, maybe adding motorbikes to carry messages, but only the company that sees itself as being in transportation, rather than just taxis, could ever create the opportunity to go to the moon. The plan itself is perhaps less important than the planning; it is the *thinking* that goes into planning that makes the difference.

Even after careful planning, the marketing approach you advocate will still be something of a 'shot in the dark'. There are always unknown factors, and any clarification will help. Planning will reduce risk, even if it cannot be perfect. The consequences of not having enough information are clear. There is all the difference in the world between 'a light at the end of the tunnel' and 'a train coming towards you'. Pessimists make poor planners; seeing any light at the end of the tunnel, their reaction is to order more tunnel.

A plan that is only a budget is not enough. The plan must concentrate on *how* things will be achieved, *who* will do what, *the timing* of action and what will *not* happen. The plan must focus attention and activity on key areas. You cannot, and indeed must not, try to do everything. The extent of the product range provides a good example of this principle. Some companies have far too many products, sometimes doing justice to none because the effort and resources are spread too thinly. Relentless concentration pays off for some. Wrigley's only make one product, chewing gum, and nothing else, but they sell millions and millions of packets of it, as the pavements of most cities testify.

Whilst a company can sometimes be successful without a plan, most successful companies do plan, and successful marketing people spend time getting the plan right. Having laid plans and mounted a successful attack though, they may prefer to describe what was done as instant creative decision-making and a reflection of their inherent understanding of the market. In fact, it is a bit of both. Planning does part of the work, but decisions remain necessary, and important, as things progress.

A plan should not be overcomplicated, as it will make it easier to implement and ensure everyone's compliance. However, it does need clear objectives, and these must be helpful in a practical sense, stating:

❑ *what* will be done;
❑ *how* it will be achieved;
❑ by *whom*;
❑ *when*.

Plans should have a degree of formality and should be written documents, even in the smallest company. However, if the document ends up being like a telephone directory, either too voluminous or too dense, then, no matter how good it is, it will end up gathering dust on a shelf and not influence the business positively at all. The key points in making planning effective are to be certain that:

❑ all the objectives set are clearly related to specific actions and people, and that lesser actions do not get in the way;
❑ priorities are flagged and staff throughout the organization know what these are, so that action at every level is accurately directed towards agreed objectives;
❑ all activities in the plan can be measured, assessed, and controlled to enable fine-tuning as the year and the plan progress.

WHY A PLAN IS NECESSARY

Every firm regardless of size should have a plan. It is nothing more or less than a ruler indicating how the firm measures up in the business world. If a firm is to improve, it must know its business standing within the marketplace, as otherwise it will not know if it is improving – and any firm that is not getting better is getting worse. There must be a will to succeed and not just scrape through. To do well is important. Standing still is not an option. The plan guides all future action and directs the business activity.

What assistance the plan can provide

The marketing plan acts as a bridge between the firm and the outside world, its markets and customers. Both sides of this bridge must be secure before it is safe to cross over and seek to achieve the business objectives that have been set. Without a plan everything is done on an *ad hoc* basis, and the company may lurch forward from crisis to crisis. We have probably all seen aspects of this in our business lives in firms with which we deal. One small problem overlooked in planning can lead to chaos. Sometimes it seems that people never learn from their problems, because similar things happen time and time again. It is no way to run a company or even part of it; it is just crisis management, reacting to every small bump along the road to success. With a proactive organization, many of these bumps will already have been foreseen and included in the scheme of events. This gives the business a smoother ride and leaves time for the inevitable few potholes that *will* be met along the way.

THE PLANNING PROCESS

The process should include all those necessary to put the plan together. It is not an exercise to be got out of the way by one person, or even one department, burning the midnight oil. It should draw on many sources, and should subsequently be part of the communication around the organization. General involvement makes it more relevant, and more likely to be practical and therefore used.

For the market plan to be put into action, the senior management of the company need to answer four key questions:

1. Where are we now?
2. Where do we want to go?
3. How will we get there?
4. How will we know when we get there?

Individual companies will put their plan together considering size, style and many other factors, depending on what is to be achieved. There are some main issues relevant to any plan. The key aim of all long-term planning is to make the day-to-day running of the business easier, more certain and more likely to produce the desired results. The plan should be the vehicle that creates action, which in turn generates business success. Goals must be set and, perhaps above all, action plans must be in place to ensure that the right things are done at the right time. For instance, more often that you might think, brilliant advertising campaigns are run before the product is in the shops. This is often worse than the advertising being late, as the customer, having asked for the product once, may not ask again. Bringing the plan together may involve many people, from the managing director down, from the sales and marketing side of the company and from other functions such as finance, but it must be co-ordinated by whoever has overall marketing responsibility, with contributions by others. You may like to consider who is or should be involved in your company.

As was stated in Chapter 1, if we look at the business through the customer's eyes and ask the question, 'What do we need to do to satisfy our customers?' then the answer should be in our plan. This question takes us beyond mere products, and applies equally to old as well as to new (to us) untapped markets. It is all too easy to become myopic and only see what the company currently sells. The danger is that, as market needs change, they are not recognized as having changed. There will always be a certain amount of market lag, but if we are too late to exploit change, others will establish a lead. The answer is to try to be aware of market changes. What starts out as a niche market can very quickly turn into a segment, and then eventually dominate the market. Look, for example, at the way personal computers have grown over the last couple of years. Look regularly at all the unfulfilled needs of your market, and examine all segments and the most profitable niche markets. The market will lead you to the areas requiring attention. The plan must reflect how action should be incorporated to take advantage of change.

Next let us consider what should be integral to the plan. Planning is a rolling process, working within a progressively changing situation, updating, revising and accommodating change in a dynamic marketplace so that progress continues smoothly, and there are as few surprises along the way as possible. The marketing plan should:

❑ contain a statement of assumptions about economic, techno-logical, social and political developments (both long- and short-term);
❑ review the sales and profit results of the company (by product or product category, market and geographical breakdown);
❑ analyse opportunities and threats;
❑ analyse internal strengths and weaknesses, and compare them with those of the competition (a chart can be useful here);
❑ review long-term objectives with regard to growth, financial return, etc, to see if achievements are on target;
❑ ask whether the next review period objectives need to be changed;
❑ set out timed specific marketing activity – what will be done, and in what order – allowing co-ordination of various elements;
❑ review the link with the intended longer-term plan (typically 3 or 5 years, though some heavy industries need longer, and certain Japanese companies talk of 100-year plans!);
❑ identify priorities for action linked to opportunities and action specified if not already in hand (it may be as worth while to state what will *not* be done as to say what will, so that activity is focused rather than dissipated).

KEEP IT MANAGEABLE AND ENSURE IT IS PRACTICAL

The following should help ensure practicality:

❑ *Market focus*: All individuals involved in the marketing process need to be taken into account. All relevant information should be assessed, and no stone left unturned in ensuring that the plan is based on sound, complete and up-to-date information. The result must be market-based: the plan should set out what we believe the market will allow us to do, not an idealized vision that would be convenient internally, but simply would not work for customers.

❑ *Time allocation*: Planning takes time. Other pressures always intrude but, unless done thoroughly, it may not be worth doing at all. Start far enough ahead, make the time and insist others involved do likewise.

❑ *Systematic approach*: Some sort of system is needed. The formats and approaches used should be sensibly standardized throughout the organization. Planning demands a plan! In other words, the complete process needs to be set out and communicated if everything is to come together and prove useful.

THE BUDGET LINK

While plans are not budgets, they must include them. This is not the place to set out every detail of budgeting, which is a whole separate subject. Let us end this chapter by saying that the financial side of the plan must be well thought out, properly calculated and clearly documented. Marketing sees its expenditure as an investment. Others may take a different view of the amounts to be spent and the risk, or may simply prefer to see expenditure go on something else.

The plan must justify the cost of the action. Make it clear to all what will be done and what will result in a way that inspires confidence. Certainly whoever is in charge of marketing should have confidence in the plan, and in making it work.

4

POSITIONING FOR BETTER RESULTS

THE PRODUCT OR SERVICE AND ITS POSITIONING IN THE MARKET

Products need names. In the good old days, it was sufficient to give them the name of the inventor or manufacturer, for example Smith's Crisps. If you could not find a name (so cartoons tell us), Acme would do. Today the brand name is expected to say something about the product and be part of creating its cachet value. This is all part of creating an image for the product that sets it apart from other products of its type, so people will prefer to buy it.

With major brands (especially of consumer products), agencies are often employed, and this applies in particular if the product is going to be launched internationally. Everything should be carefully considered, for example whether the name is catchy, easy to pronounce and looks good on the pack, and whether it will work in a foreign language (or will have some unfortunate meaning – like the car company that wondered why their car called Nova was not selling in Mexico, until someone informed them that Nova meant 'no go' there). It is important to get it right first time, as you might not get a second chance; changing horses mid-stream can be complex and expensive. If you have a superb product but the public perception is that it is inferior, any aspect contributing to this view (such as the name, packaging – whatever) must be changed. This has happened so many times in the past that companies are prepared to spend that bit extra to make sure the public get the right impression. It is even better if they have an impression that the product is better than it actually is ('hype').

THE RIGHT POSITION

Brand or product positioning is the position of a particular brand on a scale of similar competing brands, and determines how high or low a price should be set for it, how popular or exclusive an image should be aimed for, and how practical or fashionable it will appear.

How do you find your optimum position in the market? Probably most people approach it in a similar way to approaching the boss for a rise – asking for a little more than they expect, but not so much as to be counter-productive. Positioning is not a once and for ever situation; it can be altered progressively, for example at the time of a price increase or decrease.

As far as a product's being popular or exclusive is concerned, the exclusive lines generally cost more, and you are likely to make more profit per item, but the popular line will usually make more total revenue. The exclusive line may give a profit bonus, as often it will cost the same to manufacture and distribute as the more popular line.

Positioning with regard to being practical or fashionable also needs to be considered. Fashionable things tend to be more ephemeral, and indeed may have obsolescence as part of the design to make customers want the subsequent model. This can be seen with motor cars where, when a new model is launched, the following model is often already at the prototype stage. It may well only be a face-lift model with the same running gear, engine, suspension, etc as the existing model, but designed to create impact in the marketplace. The same thing can be seen with mobile phones and in the white goods market, with washing machines, for instance, where there is such a proliferation of models that comparison is made almost impossible.

PRODUCT IMAGE

Every organization must ask itself what people think of it and, if it has thought about that question, seek to maintain a positive image or create a better image than the current one. An organization's product image is an extension of the image of the organization itself, and can be powerfully descriptive. Think what a clear, detailed picture comes to mind of some companies just from the mention of their name: Sainsbury's, Sony, or Siemens for instance. On analysis, the image conjured up is often subjective rather than based on detailed factual knowledge. It is the sum of all the feelings and emotions that go with the name, and can be very fragile. Even the best reputation can change markedly and rapidly, for example Marks and Spencer. Possibly the worst example of bad press in Britain recently has been with Perrier water. Quality concerns turned them from market leader to being almost nowhere overnight. This left a market vacuum that many small British companies have turned to their advantage.

Companies work hard at creating the right image, one of a unique product, to give it a perceived 'added value' but, as there are in reality very few unique products, the trick is to make the public *think* that the product is unique. Image might be linked to advanced engineering (on, say, a Volvo motor car, making it safer), or to something more vague (as with an enhanced version of a washing powder now having 'Z 2000'). Whatever the link, it must be important to the customer. Concept and reality have little to do with each other in this game. 'Brand image' is how customers see the total product range, or even a single product, relating to *themselves*. It is usually at its strongest with high-value prestige items, where extra effort with product differentiation can be turned into extra profit. Image is well worth promoting for products such as BMW cars or Rolex watches, but not worth promoting so much with homogeneous products like bags of potatoes or commodities such as gas oil for tractors. There are middle-image products such as biscuits or hair shampoo where, because of the volume sold, product differentiation can make a big difference to the company's bottom line.

What creates a good product image, and how can it be enhanced? There are many disparate things – products, people, packaging – that can affect this, and they have a cumulative effect. All are important to public perception. Even such things as the quality of the way the switchboard handles telephone calls, or the way the receptionist (often the same person) deals with clients, are vital. Creating good first impressions is very important for most companies, and it amazing how often even large companies let themselves down by choosing the wrong people for such roles. It was Oscar Wilde who said, 'Only fools don't judge by appearances', and this is advice worth remembering in all aspects of marketing.

Letterheads and business cards, staff appearance and service all help to build the image of the company. In many firms a poster can be seen, showing a picture of a lion, which bears the logo, 'The customer is king'. This is a constant reminder to staff, and something worth remembering for everyone in marketing.

Better marketing is only possible if you have a clear idea of how you are perceived at any particular moment. Perception surveys can be used, but they have to be carefully worded or a negative conclusion may be drawn, wrongly. Such research can be costly, but just keeping your ear to the ground is often as useful and, by balancing compliments and complaints, will let you know what the public think.

Consider any large company, one of which you have no direct experience, and think of your perception of it. Ask yourself why you have this perception. Your opinion will come largely from what it tells you about itself, which to a great degree comes from advertising and other promotional activity. Advertising is, by definition, 'any paid form of non-personal communication directed at target audiences through various media in order to present and promote products, services and ideas' or, more simply, 'salesmanship in print or film'. Sponsorship is a specialized form of advertising, which is linked to something else, usually sport or music. It can greatly enhance the product image and the company's reputation, as well as putting large sums of money into areas that might die without it. It is difficult to imagine the manufacturers of sports trainers existing without the link to sport itself. All such activity, whatever else it aims to achieve, is part of what builds image and thus realizes a company's positioning objectives.

Before leaving this section, let us remember who first told us that Rolls-Royce made the finest cars in the world. It was Rolls-Royce. If you tell people something often enough and can back it up, then you have a reasonable chance of being believed. That, in a nutshell, is what makes positioning work.

BRANDING

The idea behind the branding of products is the same as that behind the branding of cattle. It is to identify them as yours and, in the case of products and services, to encourage customer loyalty. This identity can work both ways, and customers may use a product because they wish to identify with the particular lifestyle it represents. They may wish to appear richer or more successful than they are, so will opt for the accoutrements of conspicuous consumption. It has often been said that the drivers of certain makes of cars are similar people; but who chooses? Did the producer target the correct group of customers, or did the customers identify with people who drive that make of car? Probably it is a bit of both. Can we say that if a product brand does not relate to all customers it has failed? Not necessarily. Perhaps the product was not aimed at everyone in the first place. For instance, however much advertising, strategic thinking or market research is carried out, the sales of aftershave products for women will remain strictly limited. So it is possible – indeed often necessary – to target specific groups of people for specific products. You do not try to sell Rolls-Royces in the minicar market; you need to tailor your product to its market.

Every aspect of presentation is important. For example, packaging can act very strongly in brand identification. It works as an advertisement and, if you get it right, it should give added value to the product. It is taken for granted that packaging should keep the product secure, and safe in transit, and should allow it to stack neatly without falling over, but producers want it to do more. Packaging is taken so seriously by manufacturers that sometimes it can cost more than its contents.

PRODUCT DEVELOPMENT

Nine out of ten new consumer products fail within the first two years and, as there are very few, truly new products, it may be as well to consider what a new product really is. Sometimes it has good tangible advantages, and sometimes there are small changes or just repackaging. Whatever the change, the product launch is an important event for the company, and will need careful planning and execution. Positioning, after all, starts at the product launch stage. The first job is to create a new concept and, if the changes are few, and the mass marketing of it will be expensive, then getting the right message over is a major issue.

Consider, for example, a piece of capital equipment. Getting it to market may require years of research and development (R&D), together with a substantial marketing programme. Indeed sometimes research and development facilities are required just to keep pace with current developments, and their loss for even a year may lead to a company having to leave the market. The function of research and development is to improve and develop products to give a marketing advantage. This does not always work, as the Mark 2 version may not be better than the previous model or than the next competitor's model (and they have doubtless been using their own R&D facilities). Usually, though, R&D will extend the brand life of a product and therefore greater profit will be made.

Sometimes a product can, say, be made more powerful by fitting a larger motor, adapted for another use or even turned into something else, all giving opportunities for extra profit. There are also times when a product may appear completely new but the changes are in fact cosmetic, for example when the top bodywork of a car has been changed but the same floorpan, engine and running gear as in the previous model have been used. The important point is that the customer should perceive, and like, the difference.

When the new product is agreed, detailed project management takes over. The product must be launched in a fully co-ordinated fashion. For example, when the advertising campaign breaks, the production department must be able to handle the demand, products must be in stock with the retailers and communications like press coverage must link in on time. Any mismatch can cause problems, possibly failure, with the reasons only being discovered later.

Every aspect of the marketing process can contribute to successful positioning. Even something as seemingly simple as a slogan is important. A unique form of words – like Coke's 'The Real Thing' – can augment a product's marketing disproportionately. The same principle applies to more generic descriptions or phrases. There was a time some years ago when 'new' was never used without 'improved' – indeed over a period this became the norm. Then the use of the two words together became tired and, more importantly, seemed like a hackneyed old expression. Something fresher was required – and will be again and again.

A technique that can reduce the risk of failing to establish a new product with the right positioning is test marketing, which is used especially with consumer products. It usually takes the form of a limited launch in a restricted geographical area where customers fit the required profile. Costs are kept low until success seems assured, and then the full launch can go national or international. One thing is certain: the competition will follow every phase closely and try to minimize the product's success. Customers may also be suspicious, fickle, or even uninterested; this often depends on how well the market research was conducted or how well the test was set up. In some industries, for example consumer goods such as toiletries, launching a new product is a regular event, but in capital industries where development times are extended, it may be a rare event. Success is never guaranteed, but the rewards of getting it right are high.

It will not happen, however, without one other factor being considered: that of price.

THE ROLE OF PRICE IN CREATING IMAGE

With any product you care to mention, its price and image are inextricably linked, which has a direct bearing on how successful the product will be – and importantly on how much profit it will generate.

So do customers want the cheapest product? 'Yes' may be the obvious answer, but not if the product is 'nasty'. What customers really want is 'VFM' – value for money. This means they are prepared to pay more for products of superior quality, and it applies whatever the product sold. Rolls-Royce and the word 'cheap' just do not go together. The consumer expectation is that a Rolls-Royce will command a Rolls-Royce price, and indeed a virtue is made out of it by referring to other products as 'the Rolls-Royce of X' and charging accordingly. Many producers use this expectation openly in their offering. The Belgian beer Stella Artois is sold as 'reassuringly expensive'.

How do you arrive at the right price? Well, the price must be reasonable. Customers may well say, 'Your "reasonable" and my "reasonable" may not be the same'. This is true, of course, but, within limits, you can judge what the market will bear, taking into account the market segment and the level of competition. Now you have a framework for deciding if there is a hole in the market that could be filled at a profit, and if it is worth doing the necessary calculations to see if that would be desirable.

PRICE AND PROFIT

What people think of the price is only part of the picture and, as shown earlier, does not necessarily determine whether they will buy. There are four basic approaches to determining price, and these are shown below:

1. *Cost-plus pricing*: This takes all the costs of a product, plus a margin for profit, to arrive at the selling price.
2. *Market-demand-based pricing*: This looks at price from the point of view of demand. A high demand means that a higher price can be achieved and a lower demand means the reverse. Demand dictates the 'elasticity of the price'. The classic case to illustrate this is that of the railway companies. The supply of trains is limited, and few rival companies can enter the field. The result is that demand exceeds supply, and so railway companies charge what the market will bear – ask any commuter.
3. *Competition-based pricing*: This relates a particular company's price to the price of similar products in the marketplace. It allows the price to be set intentionally higher, lower or on a par with the competition.
4. *Marketing-based pricing*: This only considers the marketing view. Its aim is to set the price in such a way as to produce value satisfaction in customers. It can be influenced by:
   – all aspects of the company including its product and service;
   – status, for example endorsements by opinion leaders, exclusivity or promotion;
   – price barriers operating in a segment.

In the situation where competition does not influence price, it may be too easy to overprice your product, though it is possible to do the reverse.

The four structures above are not mutually exclusive, and elements of each plus other factors need to be considered in the overall pricing policy. If one element is underrated, then the price may be out of kilter with the marketplace, losing either profit or sales. However, this is not a once-and-for-all situation, and can be reviewed and altered.

There is a further element that has entered pricing recently, which is confusion pricing: it is regrettably something that is happening more and more, especially with railways and mobile phones. The prices set are so complex that they cannot be easily compared to the competition, so consumer choice is effectively limited. This may work for a while, but there is always the danger of a consumer backlash or of competitors setting themselves apart from what is happening in the industry and achieving differentiation.

Many techniques for using price exist, all designed to get better impact from the marketing power of pricing. 'Two for the price of one' is just one example. Sometimes called 'BOGOF' ('Buy one, get one free') it is something offered by many – sometimes to shift stock, sometimes as part of a plan linked to promotion.

Pricing can be used strategically. With 'skimming', high prices are set when there is little competition, to maximize sales from initial purchases. This happens in, amongst others, the computer and other fast-changing technological equipment markets. Similarly, 'penetration pricing' aims to increase sales by setting a lower and highly competitive price, thereby maximizing profit through higher volume sales. Pricing can also be set low for a period, and then returned to a higher price, something often done in the fuel oil market.

PSYCHOLOGY OF PRICE AND CUSTOMER REACTION TO IT

We saw earlier how price is an important, but not the only, consideration of a sale, so how do you make sure that you maximize price without losing sales? Anyone knowing the answer to that one, every time, would be a millionaire. It does vary so much from product to product and, to a certain extent, the goal posts are always moving, as it is a dynamic market. Consider this example. Having done all your research, you launch your product at a certain price on the market. You find the market has an energy of its own and, because the take-up has been so good, you start having difficulty keeping up with production. This is a classic situation and has happened many times in the past. You are now faced with the decision whether you should raise the price to dampen down the market and maximize profit. Before making the decision, you must assess the likelihood of a price increase damaging the consumer's expectation of the new product and, perhaps, starting a price war.

Many situations that demand pricing decisions are more complex than this and demand wide review of all factors before a decision is made. However, a decision does have to be made even if it is to do nothing and get round the problem another way. Your relationship with your new customers could be damaged, and a bad piece in the press could kill the product. It is not necessary to look far to find many such examples. Wrong pricing tactics can cause damage to the brand image, especially to brands at the top end of the market, and may cause a price war that is difficult to stop. There is no one as fickle as the customer.

The exact price also needs consideration: £9.99 and £49.99 are popular prices, whereas £10 and £50 are not. This goes for a host of other prices, and even for car prices at £9,999. These barrier prices seem very strong with customers, and the reason is not entirely clear. Research shows that such pricing has great appeal, especially with women, and sells more products than round-figure pricing. Having said this, many consumers find it difficult to recall the price they have paid for products, especially if they consider them low-cost items. Attitudes to pricing structures can and do change. Influenced by fashion and a preference for a more open and honest approach, there is evidence of a reversion to round-figure prices. This may last for a while until something else is tried. It is best not to try to rationalize this phenomenon, but it is further ammunition you can use.

Pricing is a complex issue, one that needs careful consideration from both the marketing end and the customer end. Get it right, and marketing is likely to work better in every respect; but there are dangers and every aspect needs careful consideration.

CREATING POWERFUL PRODUCT PROFILES

Just the silhouette of a Coca-Cola bottle is immediately recognizable as a brand to most people in the world (indeed 'Coca-Cola' is the most recognized English phrase world-wide after 'OK').

The company used several different designs over the years before arriving at the present shape. It works now, but who can say what the public will want in 10 years' time? It is such a powerful design currently that other products, which have nothing to do with soft drinks, use its shape and logo, and this has resulted in its becoming an art form in its own right. How did all this happen? It was certainly no accident, but a cumulative process affected by many things: shape, logo and colour all played their part. The company worked very hard over the years to project the correct brand image, and their success was reinforced by a very considerable advertising budget. Incidentally, it is believed that more millionaires have been made amongst those involved in this product's chain of marketing activity than in any other.

Image design may be linked to the fashion of the moment, or it may be distinctive on its own, as with Swatch watches and Swatch's 'Smart' cars, produced through their link to Mercedes Benz. The artist will see the design in its own right but, from a commercial point of view, customers want things to be functional, so looking good and performing well should go together.

Some companies always seem to have been there, constant and never changing, for example Bovril and Electrolux. Powerful images have perhaps been cleverly created, because in reality the companies have not appeared as if by magic, but have been evolving all the time. The company that is standing still is actually going backwards. Image is always fragile. It may be that, in the acquisition of companies to form a group, the specific image of a company known for its excellence in a certain field gets watered down. Then the image-makers have to build on what they already have and, without losing anything, build it into something bigger. It is no mean feat and does not always work, especially if the group is constantly changing.

So what are the actions that ensure a powerful product profile? Some organizations with a high profile are well established and constantly evolving. The job for them is to build on and extend their success. Others may be starting from scratch because they are new, or launching new products or projects that must be given an appropriate initial positioning. All must:

❑ have a clear positioning strategy, based on sound analysis;
❑ give attention to every detail that creates the customer perception the chosen positioning demands;
❑ link marketing activity in all its forms to the strategy;
❑ regard the process of creating and maintaining the positioning as dynamic (in other words, this job never ends, but what needs to be aimed at and accomplished, changes).

Better marketing always involves sound positioning; and perhaps better positioning is one of the keys to better marketing.

5

GETTING TO MARKET

For all that marketing demands must be done within the organization, activity must also link to the market, not just in terms of
focusing on customers and their needs, but literally. You have to
move goods and services to market and create direct contact with
buyers. The process that allows this to happen is *distribution*.

Let us take general principles first. However good the product
or service, however well promoted and however much customers
– and potential customers – want it, it has to be got into a position
that gives them easy access to it: it must be distributed. This can
be a complex business. A great variety of potential methods makes
it a marketing variable, albeit one that many regard as rather more
fixed than it in fact is. Consider the ways in which goods are made
available. Consumer products are sold in shops (retailers), which
vary enormously in nature, from supermarkets and department
stores to specialist retailers, general stores and more, even market
traders. These may, in turn, be variously located: in a town or
city centre, in an out-of-town shopping area, in a multi-storey
shopping centre, or on a neighbourhood corner site.

The complexity does not stop there. Retailers may be supplied
by a network of wholesalers or distributors, or they may not be
involved at all – some consumer products are sold direct, by mail
order, door-to-door, or through home parties (like Tupperware).
A similar situation applies to services, with even traditional
banking services being made available in stores, from machines
in the street and through post and telephone – even on a drive-in
basis.

Banking is an example of the changes going on in the area of distribution, many of these developments being comparatively recent moves away from traditional branch operations. They may be driven by the need to reduce costs, but will only succeed if they create new ways of doing things that *prove acceptable to customers* or, better still, that customers come to like better than what went before. Business-to-business industrial products and services are similarly complex in the range of distributive options they use.

THE ELECTRONIC REVOLUTION

There are currently many changes in areas linked to computer technology and the Internet. New words, 'e-commerce', 'e-tailing' and so on, are entering the language. They describe very new ways of doing things, some radically different from the old. This warrants its own chapter (see Chapter 10), so more details are left until then. Here it should perhaps be noted that one effect of the whole change may be that distribution comes to be regarded as easier. More changes may occur here in the future and the rate of such change may increase. Marketing must be ahead of the game, and look continuously for opportunities to create better ways of doing things.

Leaving that on one side we return, for the moment, to more conventional distribution.

DECISIONS ABOUT DISTRIBUTION

Areas where change has occurred, or is occurring, can prompt rapid customer reaction if the new means being offered are found to be convenient. Old habits may die hard, but if change is made attractive and visible, then new practices can be established that can quickly become the norm. Conversely, if the distribution method is inconvenient for customers, they will seek other ways to access the product (or simply not buy it). Sometimes inconveniences are tolerated because need is high or because they are compensated for by other factors. For example, people will put up with queues in one shop if the alternative is too far away, or does not have convenient parking.

Many different methods may coexist as, for example, with the way a holiday can be bought at a travel agent, direct with an airline, through a telephone call centre or via the Internet.

How a company analyses its distributive possibilities and organizes so as to utilize a chosen method or methods effectively is certainly important to overall marketing success. Analysis can be assisted by the process of 'market mapping', which looks graphically at the range of options and the different routes available or in operation. It highlights the complexities and links and chains involved, and enables decisions to be made about which routes (or channels) should be used, which should be of most importance and which most marketing effort should go to support.

The example shown in Figure 5.1 relates to books and the publishing industry. It shows the way in which this kind of analysis can be done and how it lays out the possibilities for action, allowing review and fine-tuning of the action selected. This example is chosen partly because it involves the latest developments in online shopping with the likes of Amazon.co.uk (on which you should find this book!).

An organization can spread effort right across the map, or leave some channels to concentrate on others. Some distribution methods are direct, others indirect.

THE ROLE OF DISTRIBUTORS

There are, in fact, a number of good reasons for delegating this essential element of the marketing mix, for example:

❑ Distributive intermediaries provide a ready-made network of contacts that would otherwise take years to establish at what might be a prohibitive cost; even a large company might balk

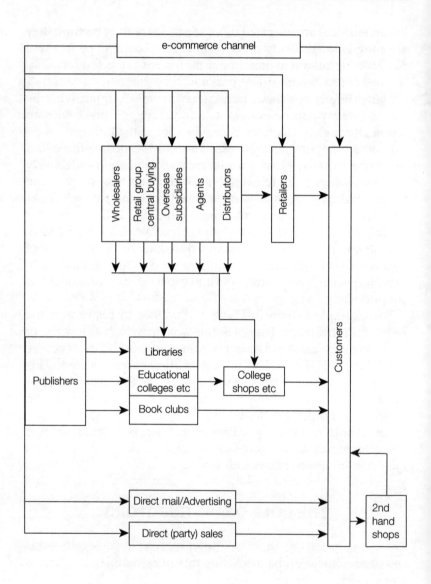

Figure 5.1 Market map

at the thought of setting up its own chain of specialist shops, and the incidence of this is very low.

❑ Distributors are objective and not tied to one product. They can offer a range that appeals to their customers, electing to pitch either wide or narrow (and there are some shops that sell very narrow, specialist ranges, eg only ties, books on sport, or coffee).

❑ Distributors provide an environment the customer needs in order to make a choice. If different competing brands need to be compared, then the customer in the store can conveniently do this. If a distributor stocks a product, and is also well known in its own right with an attractive image, this may enhance the overall attractiveness of the experience in the eyes of the consumer because of association. In many fields, allowing potential customers to view a wide choice – say, when selecting a television set – is an important aspect of encouraging sales.

❑ Distributors can spread the costs of stocking and selling one product over all the items they carry, thereby distributing it at a lower cost than could a supplier operating alone.

❑ The cost of bad debts is sometimes lower than it would be otherwise, as the distributor effectively shares the risk (however it may seem sometimes! – slow payment seems endemic in so many industries).

❑ Since the distributor is rewarded by a discount on the selling price, no capital is tied up in holding local stocks, though overlong credit can dilute this effect.

❑ Distributors have good specialist knowledge of retailing or distribution, which the principal may not possess (or they should have – this varies across different kinds of retailer, so it is important to choose well).

So far, so good, but (there is always a but) there can be conflicts of interest between principals and distributors for the following reasons:

❑ Distributors are not as committed to a particular product as its producer is. If the customer prefers another, distributors will substitute it. For example, if a customer asks for advice – 'I want to arrange a weekend break and I see there are some good deals in France' – he or she is just as likely to end up going to the Channel Islands. Agents have no particular axe to grind in selling one destination rather than another, and in some cases discount structures may lead them to make particular recommendations that benefit them rather than the buyer.

❑ Distributors may use the manufacturer's product for their own promotional purposes, something that is often linked to price cutting; not every manufacturer with a product whose price is cut wants it (a manufacturer may feel it dilutes image, but be powerless to stop it being done).

❑ Distributors may drop the product from their list if they believe they can make a better profit with another line, which will clearly affect directly competing lines.

❑ Many distributors expect the manufacturer to stimulate demand for the product, for example by advertising or providing display material. Sometimes they are more interested in the support than the product itself.

❑ Many distributors are tough on terms ('draconian' is a word one hears regularly from some suppliers!) and have complex ordering procedures. At the same time, they distance themselves from collaboration that could perhaps increase sales for both parties. (With chains, significant decisions are 'made at HQ' and sales representatives are left dealing in individual stores with young, inexperienced staff who do not know whether it is Tuesday or breakfast. This is an exaggeration, of course – well, a little.)

The question of whether to deal direct with the consumer is, therefore, dependent first upon the availability of suitable distribution channels and distributors' willingness to add additional products to the range they sell, and second on balancing the economies of the distributors' lower selling and servicing costs with the disadvantages of not being present at the point where customers are making their decisions, and thus having less control over the selling process. Realistically, many companies have no option but to go through existing external channels (whether these involve shops or not), though exactly how this is done and the mix involved can be varied. In addition, more radical variants may need to be found and run alongside (and without alienating) the retail chain; this can certainly be a way of increasing business.

SELECTING AN APPROPRIATE CHANNEL OF DISTRIBUTION

Although this is, as we have seen already, a decision involving some complex, interlocking issues, six main factors will influence the route taken:

1. *Customer characteristics*: Distributors are generally required when customers are widely dispersed, there are many of them and they buy frequently in small amounts. This is certainly true of many sectors of everyday products, less so or not at all with regard to more specialist items.
2. *Product characteristics*: Direct distribution is required when bulky or heavy products are involved. Bulky products need channel arrangements that minimize the shipping distance and the number of handlings *en route*; even a brief look at physical distribution costs shows the importance of this factor. Where high unit value can cover higher unit selling costs, then any manufacturer can keep control over distribution by dealing direct, as with certain off-the-page distribution systems, or at the far end of the spectrum door-to-door selling. Finally, products requiring installation or maintenance are generally sold through a limited network, such as sole agents.
3. *Distributor characteristics*: Distributors are more useful when their skills of low-cost contact, service and storage are more important than their lack of commitment to one product or brand. If very specific support is necessary, other options may be preferred.

4. *Competitive characteristics*: The channels chosen may be influenced by the channels competitors use, and there may be dangers in moving away too far and too fast from what a market expects and likes. This competitive interaction between retailers is another variable. In the area of fast food, Burger King tries to obtain sites near to McDonalds. On the other hand, some manufacturers, such as Avon Cosmetics, choose not to compete for scarce positions in retail stores and have established profitable door-to-door direct-selling operations instead. Similarly, major retail chains may seek to open branches near existing smaller, independent retailers, not only to take advantage of their market knowledge, but with the aim of replacing them altogether. This last may well not be in customers' interests, and illustrates one aspect of the sheer power of major retailing groups.

5. *Company characteristics*: The size of a company often correlates with its market share. The bigger its market share, the easier it is to find distributors willing to handle the product. Even a small shop is likely to find a corner for major brands, and will be selective about what else it stocks. It may not be able to stock everything, but will find space for anything it believes in, and for which there is a proven demand. Where there is clearly profit to be made, no one wants to miss out on it. Similarly, a supplier may be innovative (or may build on a strength) and seek ways of becoming less dependent on the normal chain of distribution. Creativity may have a role to play here. For instance, cosmetics may sell well in outlets that simply display them, but a store putting on make-up demonstrations (or letting the manufacturer do so) may create an edge – for a while at least. Additionally, a policy of fast delivery is less compatible with a large number of stages in the channel, and there is a danger that slow delivery (measured in market terms) dilutes marketing effectiveness. As service standards increase, so there is less scope for anyone who lags behind to do as well as might otherwise have been the case – slow delivery is increasingly not accepted.

6. *Environmental characteristics*: Changes in the economic and legal environment can also bring about changes in distributive structures. For example, when the market is depressed, manufacturers want to move their goods to market in the most economic way. They therefore cut out intermediaries or unessential services to compete on price, and deal direct.

Overall trends within retailing also influence how things are done. Out-of-town shopping, the use of the car (or restrictions on it), and everything from rental cost to the desirability of an area influence the likelihood of shoppers patronizing that area, and any particular shop in the area. This may influence where all sorts of products are bought, and this in turn may influence what is bought.

An example is the development of Covent Garden market in London. Now an attractive area of restaurants and entertainment as well as shops, it attracts people from far and wide. They might well buy something, a present perhaps, in a shop there, choosing something different from what they might have bought if they had shopped somewhere else. Such decisions are based on what is there, how it is displayed and more.

A major retailing trend is towards out-of-town shopping centres of various sorts. In some, small independent shops fit in well. In others, groups of the big retail groups (Sainsbury's, Dixons, etc) predominate, and the environment is not right for the small shopkeeper. The bigger the environmental change, the more likely it is to have repercussions. There are doubtless plenty of changes still to come in this area.

Usually it is possible to identify several different types of channel or distributors. In certain industries, some of the alternatives may be further from standard practice than others, but that does not mean they are not worthy of consideration, or cannot be part of the distribution mix. Things that are normal now may originally have been difficult to establish. For example, many in business know and deal with Wyvern Books, which sells business titles, like this one, by direct mail, sending tiny cards in packs of 20–30 in one envelope. Such promotion had not been done in this way before. It was viewed with scepticism by some people involved at the outset. However, not only does it work well, but the number of cards included in one 'shot' has grown since its inception and sales with it, as the new form of distribution has become established. Some companies are, of course, bound to the standard form in their field, but the point here is that it pays to remain open-minded. Channels may change little and traditional routes remain the most important, creating the greatest volume of business, but other possibilities may still create some growth.

There are still without doubt many possible innovations in prospect for distribution (the Internet to name but one of current interest), and things that seem unlikely today will no doubt be looked on in years to come as entirely normal. The trick for suppliers is to make sure that marketing time, effort and thinking go into exploring and testing new methods. This is true of most things, but distribution is a prime candidate for the very reason that many do see it as essentially static, at least in the short term. Perhaps this just means there is all the more possibility of using it to steal an edge and do better than more conservative competitors.

So, alternatives need to be explored to see which channel or combination of channels best meets the firm's objectives and constraints. However, the best choice of channel must take into account the degree to which the company can control, or at least influence, the distribution channel created.

In some fields, for example foods, many suppliers feel that they are too much at the beck and call of retailers, especially the large ones. Such large customers need careful handling. They are not just different in size, but in nature and, because of this, people with titles such as 'key account executive' are necessary to create, manage and maintain the relationships with them.

DISTRIBUTION MANAGEMENT

Not only are chosen distributors likely to work better on behalf of the manufacturer if communications, support (eg information, training and service) and motivation are good, but they will have their own ideas, and a good working relationship must be achieved if both sides are to profit from the partnership. This all takes time, and often it is easy simply to see people as suppliers, rather than as people to work with; yet the best will only be got from a market when the two parties do work, and work effectively, together. It is worth mentioning that the harder it may be to achieve this, the greater the rewards of doing so may be. In overseas markets, for instance, good communication – despite the distances – can be very valuable, and provides a basis for one supplier being seen as much better than another.

Distribution is a key element in marketing, one that is sometimes accepted by default because existing methods are regarded as fixed. Making existing arrangements work well – and seeking new or additional ones – can create further sales success. It forms a vital process that links the company to customers, and marketing activity can be made or broken by its performance; certainly marketing may be better if no stone is left unturned in this area. Leaving things to continue 'as they always have' can be fatal. The right methods of distribution must be chosen, and everyone down the line worked with actively and effectively. Amongst retailers, few will even consider taking on a new product (or taking on board any idea) unless they can be convinced the demand exists, and that it is more that an optimistic gleam in a supplier's eye. They need to know which market segment the product is aimed at and whether it fits with their customer franchise.

Working through any channel of distribution demands that:

❑ a clear policy exists;
❑ all parties have clear, understood and agreed expectations of one other, including the terms of trade (discounts and all financial arrangements);
❑ sufficient time and resources are put into the ongoing process of managing, communicating with and motivating those organizations and people upon whom sales are ultimately dependent.

There is always a range of options. Some may seem to be 'the norm', others peripheral or 'unlikely to work', and still more cannot yet be anticipated. Whatever is done, whatever range of ways is used together, distribution is an area that marketing must aim to influence. It is at the interface, whatever form that takes, where sales are made. Suppliers must work effectively with fixed processes (and this includes dealing with aspects of the business they would rather were different), and must also seek innovative and creative new approaches to distribution where appropriate, to make marketing better.

6

TELLING THE WORLD

Given a crowded and dynamic marketplace, and demanding and fickle customers, no one – even with an excellent product or service to sell – should assume that customers will buy without prompting. There is a considerable, and potentially varied, communications job to be done and it is not a one-off process, but an ongoing one.

GETTING CUSTOMERS TO BE REGULAR USERS

How do you move customers, who may start by being totally unaware of your product, to change their attitude along the way to being regular users? There are many techniques you can use, each one bringing you closer to customers and moving them towards the final goal of regular use. You can use public relations, advertising, direct mail, sales promotion and many other techniques to achieve this. There may be various objectives set for this persuasion, including getting potential customers to:

❑ try a product;
❑ buy more, or more frequently;
❑ extend the use of the product (eg eating breakfast cereal as a supper snack);
❑ develop trust in the company through one brand so that others in the range are also bought.

The sequence of customers moving from being totally unaware of your company or product to being regular users is worth looking at in some detail. Each step represents a change in attitude by the customers or prospective customers. The steps are:

1. *Unawareness to awareness*: This is the stage where prospective customers move from no knowledge of a product to where they know about it, or at least of its existence. Their attitude is receptive but passive, and their major need is information. Promotion is targeted at:
   - introducing a concept;
   - telling prospects that something more specific exists;
   - creating an automatic association between the needs of prospects and the product.
2. *Awareness to interest*: This is the move from a passive to an active stage of attention. Prospects will have their interest aroused by the product's newness or appearance, or by the concept or what is said about it. Their response can be active or passive. Promotional objectives are to:
   - gain their attention through the message;
   - create interest in the product;
   - provide a succinct summary of all the relative information prospects have.
   At this stage, all the aspects of the promotion mix begin to get prospects to say, ' I must check this product out'.
3. *Interest to evaluation*: This is when buyers first consider the effect of the product on their personal motivation, which includes image, lifestyle, circumstances, needs, etc. They go through a process of reasoning, analysing the arguments and looking for personal advantages. Depending on their needs and the price, they may look for more information or other validation of their initial impression. Prospects are now giving out buying signals so an attempt can be made to:
   - create a situation that encourages them to start this phase of reasoning;
   - discover and focus on their relevant wants and needs;
   - segment and target buyers according to their requirements.

4. *Evaluation to trial*: This is a key movement from a mental state of evaluation to the positive action of trial. The prospects' basic requirement is to try the product and evaluate the findings. Promotional objectives are to:
   - identify the usage opportunities clearly;
   - suggest a time-scale for the trial.

   In other words, the aim is to encourage the first purchase so that the buyer says, 'This does look good and does all I require. I'll buy it'.

5. *Trial to usage*: Buyers take this step if the trial has been successful. Sometimes steps 4 and 5 come together. The objectives of promotion are to:
   - provide reminders of key elements, such as brand, image and technical advantages;
   - emphasize success and satisfaction;
   - remind the buyer of other usage opportunities, and provide supporting proof via third-party references.

6. *Usage to repeat usage*: This is the final objective of the promotion, and buyers may well be going through the above stages with other suppliers. When they move from occasional usage to constant usage, they move into a state of identifying themselves with the product, and selection of the product will be automatic until something happens to upset that balance. The objectives are now simpler, though not necessarily easier to achieve, and are to:
   - maintain the climate that has led to satisfaction;
   - keep up the image;
   - maintain contact and confirm the key qualities of the product, and advise of other products as they come along.

The above sequence dissects the process in detail. Buyers may have changed from a product they have used for many years, and may well feel they are now duty-bound to try several other products, not just yours, now that their buying pattern has been upset – so be on your guard. Customers will probably not be aware of the sequence they have just gone through, and they may make very rapid progress from stage 1 to stage 6, but the sequence is real, and it is what promotion must influence.

The promotional mix of all the elements that have influenced customers along the way can be many and varied, from something small like a leaflet through the door to a major advertising campaign on hoardings. With this in mind, marketing can utilize and deploy the separate and individual techniques, making them work to achieve exactly what is wanted. It is important to bear in mind, when implementing these techniques, that the effect of each is different, and that it is difficult to separate each individual impact. People's image of an organization is the total cumulative effect of everything they see and hear about it.

THE PROMOTIONAL BUDGET

There are several approaches to the complex issue of setting a promotional budget. This section reviews them and suggests how a rational decision can be taken in this difficult area. The main approaches to setting the promotional budget are to consider:

❑ *Percentage of sales*: This takes a fixed percentage, usually based on forecast sales, and relies on the questionable assumption that there is always a direct relationship between promotional expenditure and sales. The budget is simply calculated as a percentage of sales revenue. Similarly, if for example increased sales of 15 per cent are forecast, it is assumed that a 15 per cent increase in promotional effort will also be required. This rationale may not be realistic, as it depends on many factors other than expenditure. This is probably the least effective, but the traditional and easiest approach.

❑ *Competitive parity approach*: This involves spending the same amount on promotion as your competitors, or maintaining the same proportion of expenditure as the industrial average for similar organizations. The assumption is that in this way you will retain your market share. However, your competition may have different objectives, ie their promotion is designed to do things that do not correspond to the tasks yours has, and so the costs are not comparable. If you can form a view of either the direction or the spend of competitive industry, it may be useful, but the danger is that, as this is the 'collective wisdom' of the industry, the blind may end up leading the blind! It is important to remember that competitors' expenditure cannot be more than an indication of the budget spend. For strategic reasons, it may be that your expenditure should be either greater than your competitors' to drive them out, or much less, perhaps for other reasons. Remember that no two firms pursue identical objectives from the same base line of resources, market standing, etc. It is also fallacious to assume that all competitors will spend equally or to the same effect.

❏ *Combination of percentage of sales and competitive parity*: This is a more comprehensive approach but does not overcome the inherent problems of each earlier method. It does recognize the need for profitability and takes into account the impact of competitor expenditure.

❏ *What is affordable?*: If the optimum amount of spend cannot be objectively decided, then whatever money is available will do. Therefore decide:
  – what sums are available after all costs have been accounted for;
  – the cash situation in the business as a whole;
  – the revenue forecast.

In some companies, advertising and promotion are left to share out the tail end of the budget, and more expenditure is equated with lower profits (especially where accountants reign supreme). In others, more expenditure on promotion might lead to more sales at marginal cost, which in turn leads to higher profits overall. This is not the best method, demonstrating an *ad hoc* approach that leaves out assessment of opportunities in both the long and short term.

❏ *Fixed sum per sales unit*: This method is similar to percentage of sales, except that a specific amount per unit or tonne, etc, is used, rather than a percentage of pound sales value. In this way money for promotional purposes is not affected by changes in price, which takes the enlightened view that promotional expenditure is an investment, not merely a cost.

❑ *What has been learnt from previous years?*: The best predictor for next year's budget is this year's. Were the results as forecast? What was the relationship of spend to competition? What is happening in the market and will it continue? What effect is this having, and what repercussions will it have for the future? It is important to:

– experiment in a controlled area to see if underspending or overspending is current;

– monitor results, by tracking the awareness of promotions amongst customers; this can be relatively easy, and the results of experiments with different budget levels can then be used in planning the next step (although always bear in mind that all other things do not remain equal).

❑ *Task method approach*: This recognizes the weaknesses of other approaches, and a more comprehensive four-step procedure is possible. Emphasis here is on the tasks involved in implementing a promotional strategy. The four steps are as follows:

– *analysis*: analyse the market to uncover the facts for the basis of a promotional approach utilizing opportunities and specific targets and at the same time developing a strategy;

– *determine objectives*: from this analysis, set clear short- and long-term promotional objectives for continuity and build-up of promotional impact and effect;

– *identify promotional tasks*: determine the promotional activities required to achieve the marketing and promotional objectives;

– *cost out identified promotional tasks*: what is the likely cost of each element in the communications mix and the cost-effectiveness of each element?

Next, consider what media are likely to be chosen and what the target is (eg consider the number of advertisements, leaflets, etc).

In advertising, the media schedule can easily be converted into an advertising budget by adding space or time costs to the costs of preparing the advertising material. The promotional budget is usually determined by costing out the expenses of preparing and distributing promotional material, etc. A variety of options may need to be considered, balancing greater or lesser expenditure against larger or smaller returns. In other words, the tasks must be specified and costed in real detail. With this done, a budget is firmly based. The great advantage of this budgetary approach compared with others is that it is comprehensive, systematic and likely to be more realistic. However, other methods can still be used to provide 'ball-park' estimates, although such methods can produce disparate answers, for example:

❑ We can afford £12,000.
❑ The task requires £15,500.
❑ To match the competition requires £18,500.
❑ Last year's spending was £9,500.

Note: the figures quoted are examples but can be on any scale.

The decision now becomes a matter of value judgements, making allowance for overall company philosophy and objectives. There is no tremendously accurate, mathematical, or automatic method of determining the promotional budget. The task method does however provide, if not the easiest, then probably the most accurate method of determining the promotional budget.

In a large company, or one with a substantial promotional budget, promotion will be carried out by or with an advertising agency, with certain tasks such as media buying or creative input being carried out exclusively by them. It is not necessary, nor is there space here, to explore this process in more detail, but it must be done, and done well.

PROMOTIONAL MIX AND METHODS

There is no one way, and certainly no one thing, that is right for promoting everything. 'Promotional mix' is an umbrella term. It describes a number of different techniques, and implies a plethora of combinations and ways of using them. The figure below shows how different methodologies act in different ways in respect of customers, from those having influence at a distance and being directed at large numbers of people, through to one-to-one selling (of which more later).

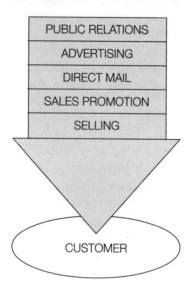

Figure 6.1 The mix of persuasive communications

A brief comment about each of the main ingredients of the communications mix will serve to put them into context at this stage.

Public relations

The aim of public relations (which encompasses press relations, also abbreviated to PR) is to create or maintain a favourable climate of opinion in which the company can operate. Every company will have an image; the question is whether it projects the right one and how strongly. It is important that the actual image reflects what is wanted.

The first task is to define those 'publics' among whom the company wants to have a favourable reputation. Having identified the target groups, the next step is to find out what image these groups currently have of the company. Do they know it and its product or service? What is their perception of both?

Some information can be obtained by keeping your ear to the ground. If this is not sufficient, more formal market research may have to be undertaken.

Once the present awareness and image have been identified, PR targets can be set, ie as to who should know and perceive what about the firm. You can then decide which PR promotional techniques will be most cost-effective in achieving the desired image goals. Typical methods include the following:

❏ *Press publicity and developing good relationships with writers and editors*: This does not just happen. It means taking the initiative, following up and delivering, sticking to deadlines, and so on (for example, telling your local radio station which person from your company would be prepared to comment at appropriate times).

❏ *Membership of influential bodies*: This also does not just happen. Someone (the right person) actually has to belong and take part. It takes time, but can lead to good contacts. Bodies such as trade associations in industries where you work or want to work should not be neglected. Contacts, once obtained, should be followed systematically, which may be as simple as arranging to ring them rather than waiting for a call that never comes.

❏ *Use of 'house style'*: This implies not just business cards and brochures, but everything from the front door and reception area to what is painted on the side of delivery trucks. Again it does not just happen; someone has to decide what is needed and how to maintain the image. Brochures are a case in point. Many brochures are the same as everyone else's: out of date, introspective, boring and – at worst – banal. A vital point to remember is that it is not just a case of making them look better (though this is important); getting the message right comes first, and a graphic designer may not be the best person to do this. It may be done better by working *with* a copywriter or consultant, though you cannot escape the responsibility of deciding *what* is said.

❏ *Public-speaking engagements*: These have to be sought out, and you have to field the right person, ie someone who can make a presentation of a quality that will get him or her asked back (not whoever is most senior or happens to be available). If done well, presentations can certainly produce enquiries. Events can range from those the organization itself puts on (promotional events) to public conferences large and small.

Advertising

Advertising – in all its many forms – is communication in bought space, the intention being to attract existing and potential cust-omers. It can:

❏ provide information;
❏ attempt to persuade;
❏ create dissatisfaction with competitive offerings;
❏ reinforce existing purchasing habits.

The mass advertising of major organizations (for example, brands promoted nightly on the television) is very familiar. For some businesses, however, limited budgets may preclude mass action, although some activity may be important. While advertising is used beneficially, especially by larger organizations, the 'best buy' in terms of promotional mix for the medium-sized firm is perhaps public relations and promotion, planned and followed through as well as reactive, coupled with an increasingly planned, organized and professional sales effort.

Direct mail

Direct mail, or promotion through the post, is essentially only a specialist form of advertising. It has considerable relevance for some firms, and is worth their detailed and separate study, as it may appear deceptively easy. In fact it must be done very carefully. Apparently minor changes to a mailshot (the total set of enclosures – letter, brochure, reply card or whatever) that goes out can make a significant difference to the response. Just adding a picture or producing a letter in two colours, for example, might make all the difference.

That said, and despite the 'junk mail' image in some quarters, direct mail is a powerful medium: it is flexible, more measurable than many promotional methods and can be tightly targeted and used on a large or small scale (100 letters or 100,000 letters).

Sales promotion

Sales promotion encompasses a number of elements, often used together as a 'campaign' around one particular product or service or at one time. Newsletters, events, briefings, etc are good examples of the kind of elements used, though any business must select what is appropriate and, of course, work only with what is acceptable to and effective with its customers. This category also includes such things as price offers, competitions, free products ('25% extra free') and many more.

Merchandising and display

These are important in retail. Everything about how a retail outlet is designed and set out is important and makes a difference. The retailer's window, the traffic flow of customers around a store, the signing – many matters can be influenced. Even the background music can make a difference. One experiment showed that supermarkets sold more German wine when German music was played! It may seem fantastic, or perhaps silly, but nevertheless, it shows something of the possibilities. The layout of Web pages is a new form of merchandising.

Sponsorship

This is again more specialized, but well known from its larger and more public manifestations such as advertising linked to major sporting events. It is used, too, across a wide range of smaller and more locally based applications.

Selling

This is somewhat different in nature, being essentially one-to-one communication. It too will not just happen, and what is done must be planned and carried out in a way that increases the chances of business resulting from it. For some it is an area of weakness. Promotional activity is often geared primarily to producing enquiries. Consider what happens when enquiries are received. People are referred to you, perhaps by an intermediary, and they telephone your business. What happens? Is the response specifically designed to give the best impression? Who speaks to enquirers? Who goes to visit them if appropriate? Is the action designed to increase the chances of business resulting, or is it dealt with by whoever is in the office that day, has time or is most senior?

To ensure success, responsibilities and even targets must be given to individuals. Sales activity must then be deployed acceptably so that, while full use is made of the techniques, customers remain content, ie so that you run the kind of customer contact you want and that customers like. See Chapter 7 for more details.

It is the totality of the mix that will bring in the business. Promotion can do a number of different things, for example:

❑ It can provide information. This information can act as a reminder to current users of the product's existence.
❑ It can attempt to persuade. This can be persuading current users to purchase again, non-users to try the product for the first time and new users to change brands or suppliers.
❑ It can create cognitive dissonance. This means advertising can help to create uncertainty about the ability of current suppliers to satisfy a need best. In this way, advertising can effectively persuade customers to try an alternative product or brand. (Extreme versions of this come under the heading 'knocking copy' – used sometimes by, among others, car manufacturers.)

❑ It can create reinforcement. Advertising can compete with competitors' advertising, which itself aims to create dissonance, to reinforce the idea that current purchases best satisfy customers' needs.

Moreover, promotion may aim to reduce the uncertainty felt by customers immediately following an important and valuable purchase, when they are debating whether or not they have made the correct choice.

MATCHING METHODS TO PURPOSE

Most promotional methods offer a range of possibilities in terms of their form. For example, consider the various kinds of advertising. These certainly vary, and each is read or seen by a different mix of people; there are advertisements on matchboxes and there has been an advertisement on the space shuttle. The possibility of finding media that correspond with the profile of the customer group you are targeting is high. For instance, there are:

❑ *Daily newspapers*: These often enjoy reader loyalty and hence high credibility. Consequently, they are particularly useful for prestige and reminder advertising. As they are read hurriedly by many people, lengthy copy may be wasted.
❑ *Sunday newspapers*: These are read at a more leisurely pace and consequently greater detail can be included.
❑ *Colour supplements*: These are ideal forums for advertising, but appeal to a relatively limited audience.
❑ *Magazines*: These vary from quarterlies to weeklies and from very general, wide-coverage journals to those of very specialized interests. Similarly, different magazines of the same type (eg fashion) appeal to different age and socio-economic groups. Magazines are normally colourful and are often read on a regular basis.
❑ *Local newspapers*: These are particularly useful for anything local, but are relatively expensive if used for a national campaign.

They are sometimes used for advertising support if you are test-marketing in one or two specific areas.

❑ *Television*: This is regarded as the best overall medium for achieving mass impact and creating an immediate or quick sales response. It is arguable whether or not the audience is captive or receptive, but the fact that television is being used is often sufficient in itself to generate trade support. Television allows the product to be demonstrated, and is useful in test-marketing new products because of its regional nature. It is very expensive.

❑ *Outdoor advertising*: This lacks many of the attributes of press and television, but is useful for reminder copy and for a support role in a campaign. Strategically placed posters near busy thoroughfares or at commuter stations can offer very effective long-life support advertising.

❑ *Exhibitions*: These generate high impact at the time of the exhibition but, except for very specialized ones, their coverage of the potential market is low. They can, however, perform a useful long-term 'prestige' role and combine advertising, promotion and sales.

❑ *Cinema*: With its escapist atmosphere, this can have an enormous impact on its audience of predominantly young people, but without repetition (eg people visiting the cinema once every week), it has little lasting effect. It is again useful for backing press and television, but for certain products only, bearing in mind the audience and the atmosphere.

❑ *Commercial radio*: This medium offers repetition, and has proved an excellent outlet for certain products. It is becoming apparent that the new local radio stations appeal to a wide cross-section of people and therefore offer 'support' potential to a wide range of products.

❑ *Web sites*: These, an aspect of the Internet revolution, are increasingly used, often as a form of advertising, sometimes linked to a facility for customers to order (the latter constituting e-commerce). As a short digression to this chapter, the boxed section sets out some key principles about the role of Web sites and how to use them.

WEB SITES

Technology has a way of creeping up on you. One day the Internet is an uncertain prediction; now we are all learning to surf, and references to e-commerce are all around. You may have bought this book by contacting a Web site (Kogan Page have one, which is: www.kogan-page.co.uk), and many businesses of all sorts, even small ones, have their own Web site. Creating something simple is now a classic low-cost option.

It is not my purpose here to explain the technology, and indeed I am hardly qualified to do so. However, a Web site is no more than a new option in the promotional mix and needs to be considered accordingly. Setting up a Web site can be time-consuming and expensive; so too can maintaining it and keeping it up to date. Some businesses acted very early as technology created this opportunity, though some acted solely because it was 'something that had to be done', perhaps to keep up with others, perhaps to pander to the ego of someone involved and enthusiastic. Whatever the reason it was sometimes ill considered, and time and money were spent to no good effect. Whatever might be done needs thinking through; the first question is very obvious and straightforward.

What objectives do you have for your Web site?

There may be several, but they should all be specific. It is important to know whether the cost of setting up a site is delivering what was intended, important not least to how the site is developed. Perhaps the site is in part a source of reference. You want people to consult it to obtain information (and be impressed by it at the same time). This may save time and effort otherwise expended in other ways. Perhaps you intend that it should play a more integral part in the selling process, and you want to measure its effectiveness in terms of counting the number of new contacts it produces and, in turn, how many of those are turned into actual revenue-producing customers.

So, if you already have a Web site, check whether you have good feedback on its use and the specific results it brings you (for example, counting new contacts or money coming from new customers). Similarly if you are in the process of setting up a site – ensure consideration of this is an inherent part of the process.

In addition, you may have products you want people to order and pay for through direct contact with the site. A consultant might offer a survey of some sort, primarily to put an example of his or her expertise and style in the hands of prospective clients (though it might also be a source of revenue). In this case not only must the ordering system work well, and this means it must be quick and easier for whoever is doing the ordering, but the follow-up must be good, too. Any initial good impression given will quickly evaporate if whatever is ordered takes for ever to arrive or needs several chasers. One hazard to good service is to demand too much information as an order is placed. Of course, this kind of contact represents an opportunity to create a useful database, but turning ordering into the Spanish Inquisition will hardly endear you to people.

Whatever objectives are decided upon, there are then three distinct tasks. They are to:

1. *attract people to the site*: Just having the site set up does not mean people will log on to it in droves, much less that the people you want to do so will act in this way. Other aspects of promotion must draw attention to it and this may vary from simply having the Web site address on your letterhead to incorporating mention (and perhaps demonstration) of it into customer events.
2. *impress people when they see it*: This applies to both its content and its presentation. It means keeping a close eye on the customers' view and the practicalities as it is set up. For example, all sorts of impressive graphics and pictures are possible, can look creative and may well impress. Certainly you will need some. But such devices take a long time to download, and if that is what you are encouraging people to do they may find it tedious, especially if the graphics seem more like window dressing than something that enhances the content in a useful way.
3. *encourage repeat use*: This may or may not be one of the objectives. If it is, then efforts have to be made to encourage

re-contacting and this too may involve an overlap with other forms of communication.

Beyond this you also need to consider carefully:

- ❏ what the content should be (this is an ongoing job, not a one-off);
- ❏ how the contacting of the Web site can prompt a dialogue;
- ❏ how topical it should be (this affects how regularly it needs revision);
- ❏ its convenience and accessibility (does it have a suitable navigation mechanism?);
- ❏ whether it will look consistent (and not as if it has been put together by committee);
- ❏ the protection it needs (whether anything is confidential or vulnerable to hackers, etc).

Overall, it will need the same planning, co-ordination and careful execution as any other form of marketing communication. In addition, it is likely to necessitate active, ongoing co-operation from numbers of people around the firm who will provide and update information. Given how difficult it can be to get even a small group of people to agree on, say, one page of copy for a new brochure, this may present quite a challenge. Clearly responsibility for the site and what it contains must be laid unequivocally at someone's door, together with the appropriate authority to see it through.

In addition, someone needs to have the knowledge that is necessary from a technical standpoint. This may be internal or external, but it needs to be linked to an understanding of marketing and/or the ability to accept a clear brief. This is not a case of applying all the available technology, and building in every bell and whistle simply because it is possible. Practical solutions are necessary to meet clear objectives.

If a site is to be useful, that is, an effective part of the marketing mix, then sufficient time and effort must be put in to get it right. The ongoing job of maintaining it must be borne in mind from the beginning.

A link with research

An interesting and practical development is the availability of standard, cost-effective software packages that can work as an integral part of a Web site and monitor how it is used. In fact, there are now such add-ons that are better described as 'research tools'. One such, ONQUEST, not only allows regular research and formal monthly analysis about exactly who is using a Web site, their precise characteristics, and how and why they are in touch with the site, but also allows the way the system works to be tailored simply to the needs and intentions of an individual firm. The intention is specifically to obtain information that will make the Web site a more accurate and effective marketing tool. (Details of the ONQUEST system can be obtained from Strategy, Research and Action Ltd (tel: 020 8878 9482). Their managing director, Robin Birn, the researcher who initiated this development, is familiar with the special nature of small business.)

Similarly, other technological possibilities come along in increasing profusion. For example, it is possible for someone logged on to a Web site to trigger a phone call from a supplier. Thus you can organize to be able to talk to potential customers as they look at your site or afterwards (they may have only one telephone line).

This whole area changes and develops as you watch. There are opportunities not to be missed but, as this short section makes clear, it needs to be approached in the right way, or effort can be dissipated without real advantage.

Note: this passage is adapted (with permission) from a small section of another Kogan Page title, Marketing on a Tight Budget *(Forsyth, 2000).*

Not all media outlets will be appropriate to the nature of any particular business. In any case, media selection is a complex subject (and best left to experts if advertising is done on any scale). You do need to consider a mix of factors however:

❏ *Cost*: The larger the exposure, the more it costs, so national daily newspapers and TV are not likely to rank high on your list. Some good rates are available on local commercial radio, however, and this may be worth investigating.

❏ *Focus*: This means by whom it will be seen. All reputable media are able to provide detailed information regarding their readership. Look for something where there is a good fit between the group(s) you want to access and those who see the media, and bear in mind that you pay for *all* the people the media addresses, so beware of those that include a much wider span of audience than you need.

❏ *Timing*: This can also be important. Some media appear regularly and you can appear pretty much when you want – in a local weekly paper, say – while others are less frequent. If timing is important to you, it is worth matching. In other words, do not easily be persuaded to advertise in, for example, a special supplement or advertising feature if its timing does not really suit you.

❏ *Production factors*: These matter too. Must your advertisement be in colour or not? Does the medium lend itself to photographs, and is this important? Will the medium itself provide assistance with design or copywriting (and is that assistance genuinely useful)?

The key issue is not whether it is readily available or whether you can afford it, but whether it will actually meet the objectives set and do the job required of it.

WHO IS THE TARGET?

It is often not enough to advertise to consumers alone. It is important that distributors are willing to stock and promote a product.

Even if the sales force plays a prime part in ensuring that stocking and promotion objectives are achieved, trade advertising also has an important role to play in this respect:

❏ It can remind distributors about the product between selling calls.
❏ It can keep distributors fully informed and up to date on developments and changes of policy.
❏ It can also alleviate the problems associated with 'cold-call' selling of less-well-known products.

Trade advertising is usually confined to specialist trade publications and direct-mail communications from the company to its distributors.

Most trade advertising occurs prior to major consumer advertising campaigns to help ensure the buying in of stock, in anticipation of future demands to be created by the consumer advertising. Thus, when new products are launched or special promotions introduced, trade support is often achieved through special offers ('13 for the price of 12') or increased (introductory) discounts, all of which trade advertising can effectively emphasize. This type of advertising can also communicate to the trade the advantage of new products, as well as the timing and 'weight' of advertising support that is to come.

Presupposing that the analysis of the market has led to a sensible choice of media and advertising strategies, these have to be communicated to whoever is going to produce the advertisement. At its best, the advertisement strategy statement is brief and economical, and does its job with regard to three issues:

❏ the basic proposition – the promise to clients, the statement of benefit, and customers targeted;
❏ the 'reason why' – support proof justifying the proposition, the main purpose of which is to render the proposition as convincing as possible;
❏ the 'tone of voice' in which the message should be delivered – the image to be projected and, not infrequently, the picture customers have of themselves, which it could be unwise to disturb, or indeed wise to capitalize on.

Putting the message together, writing the words ('copy'), selecting illustrations and so on may still be a problem. It helps to approach it in the right way. The principles are one thing; exercising them creatively is another.

If you subcontract copywriting, be careful. Most executives, when faced with a rough or initial visual and copy layout, have an automatic subjective response: 'I like it' or 'I don't like it'. While the creator may attempt to explain that the appraiser is not a member of the target audience, it is obviously difficult to be objective. Nevertheless, while an attempt at objectivity must be made, there are few experienced advertising or marketing executives who can say that their judgement has never let them down. Advertising remains as much an art as a science. The questions that you must ask are:

❑ Does the advertisement match the strategy laid down?
❑ Does the advertisement gain attention and create awareness?
❑ Is it likely to create interest and understanding of the advantages of a particular service?
❑ Does it create a desire for the benefits and conviction of the need to buy?
❑ Is it likely to prompt potential clients to action?

In basic terms, you are asking: does the advertising communicate? Will people notice it, understand it, believe it, remember it and buy it?

Quoting 'good' advertising is like walking through quicksand. In isolation from its objectives and strategy, its intention may be unclear. An advert that wins awards may sell little; a simple, unsophisticated one may achieve wonders. The following is therefore quoted (with permission) from the book *Everything You Need to Know about Marketing* (1999), written by Patrick Forsyth (also a Kogan Page paperback, and designed to demystify marketing in a light-hearted way), and takes a less-than-serious approach without using a real example (which would almost certainly be unrepresentative). This fictional advert for 'Splodge' does show something of the many different approaches possible.

SOME APPROACHES TO ADVERTISING

Sometimes the product is such that with no competition, with a perfect match with customers' needs, all the advertisement has to do is say what the product will do for them.

New instant petrol – one spoonful of our additive to one gallon of water produces petrol at 1p a gallon.

If your message is like this, no problem, persuasion is inherent in the message. But few products are like that. More likely any product will have competition – and it will be very like its competitors.

Then you have to say more about it. Or start by thinking of everything about it. You may even say everything about it:

SPLODGE – the big, wholesome, tasty, non-fattening, instant, easily prepared chocolate pudding for the whole family.

Or you can stress one factor, thus implying that your competitors' products are lacking in this respect:

SPLODGE – the easily prepared pudding.

Customers may know all puddings of this sort are easy to prepare, but they are still likely to conclude yours is easiest. The trouble with this approach is that in a crowded market there are probably puddings being advertised already as 'easily prepared'. And big, wholesome and all the rest for that matter. What then? Well, one way out is to pick another factor ignored by your competitors because it is not essential:

SPLODGE – the pudding in the ring-pull pack.

It may be a marginal factor but your advertisement now implies it is important and that the competition lacks it. Alternatively you can pick a characteristic of total irrelevance:

SPLODGE – the pudding that floats in water.

If competition has done all of this then you have only one alternative, you must feature in the advertisement something else, nothing to do with the product. This may necessitate giving something away:

SPLODGE – the only pudding sold with a *free* sink plunger.

Or re-packaging:

SPLODGE – the only pudding in the *transparent* ring-pull pack.

The possibilities are endless and the ultimate goal is always to make your product appear different and attractive, desirable because of it.

In addition, advertising has to be made to look attractive. Sometimes this may be achieved through added humour, personalities, etc, or through lavish production values – some television commercials cost far more per minute than many of the programmes they punctuate, and the photographic and editing values of the international advertising of big brands like Coca-Cola is clear to all. A danger here is that the presentation may hide the message; viewers of a poster, say, may laugh at its humour but be unable to recall what the brand name was.

CREATIVITY

Whatever else it does, all promotion must always aim to make your product or service appear different, attractive and thus desirable. Watch the advertisements on television, look carefully at what drops through your letterbox, take note of slogans and headlines, and see what appeals to you. You will notice varied standards. Promotion and advertising is not all good (because making it effective is hard to achieve), but some is memorable and much does a good job for a while.

It would not be appropriate to quote a favourite advertisement (and any quoted would quickly date); so let us end this chapter with two key points:

1. The mix must be well selected and well matched to clear purpose (promotion is not a matter of fashion or easy options).
2. Creating and implementing good promotion demands constant creative thinking and fresh approaches. Approaches do not *have* to change often (some campaigns have run in similar form for many years and work well), but they must always seem fresh. There is no end to creative ideas. What is necessary may be major, the overall essence of a whole campaign, but equally it could be one small, simple, yet significant detail that changes promotion from being routine to being special – and with it, perhaps, the sales revenue figures that are generated.

Better marketing need not mean massive promotional budgets and clever approaches, but it certainly means striking and appropriate approaches. If it does not work with customers, it does not work at all.

7

PERSONAL SELLING

Selling links with and extends promotional activity. There is an old saying that nothing happens until someone sells something, and in many businesses selling is indeed a vital part of the communications mix without which the rest of the promotional activity can be wasted. Selling is the only persuasive technique that involves direct individual personal contact.

Now selling can sometimes have an unfortunate image. Think of your own instant judgement on, say, a double-glazing or insurance salesman. The first words that come to mind may be 'pushy', 'high-pressure' or 'con man'. Selling can be associated with pushing inappropriate goods on reluctant customers. Selling refrigerators to Eskimos is perhaps the kind of situation that springs to mind (though Eskimos *do* buy refrigerators – they need them to keep food *warm* enough to cook without defrosting! But we digress).

The best – that is, most effective – selling can be described as 'helping people to buy'. Much of it has advisory overtones and, if it is to be acceptable as well as effective, it cannot be pushy, but must, like everything in marketing, be customer-orientated. Selling is, in fact, a skilled job and requires a professional approach from the field force who carry it out. Customers may want the product but, with plenty of alternative sources of supply, they are demanding, and convincing them to do business with this particular supplier may be no easy task.

In most businesses, selling must take place if the marketing process is to be successfully concluded. At one end of the scale it is simple. For example, an off-licence may be able to increase sales significantly just by ensuring that every time customers ask for spirits, they are asked, 'How many mixers do you want?' Many people respond positively to what has been called the 'gin and tonic effect', the linking of one product with another. Sometimes it is even simpler: the waiter in a hotel or bar, for example, who asks 'Another drink?' is selling.

At the other end of the scale, sales do not come from the single isolated success of one interaction with the customer. A chain of events may be involved, several people, a long period of time and, importantly, a cumulative effect. In other words, each stage, perhaps involving some combination of meetings, proposals, presentations and more meetings, must go well or you do not move on to the next.

With the thought in mind that the detail of what is necessary will vary depending on circumstances, let us review the stages in turn, together with some of the principles involved throughout the sales process.

Selling starts, logically enough, with identifying the right people to sell to. Sales time is expensive, so it is important for sales people to spend time with genuine prospects, the more so when the longer lead time typical in the purchase of, say, computer systems is involved. Some of the right people come forward as a result of promotional activity. They phone up, return a card from a mailshot or whatever and, in so doing, are saying, 'Tell me more'. Others have to be found; finding them is the first stage of the selling process.

PROSPECTS – THE PROCESS OF LOCATION

This part of the process (which overlaps to some extent with the area of marketing and promotion) is perhaps best described by way of a simple, everyday example.

Consider the manager of a successful retail travel-agency business. He identifies that, in addition to selling to customers over the counter, he is well placed to deal with commercial accounts in the area in which his business is located. He needs to initiate some contacts, but with whom? The first stage is to check. He looks at his files for companies he has dealt with previously and individual customers who work for the right kind of company. This produces some names, but he needs more and considers a list of sources including:

❑ local chambers of commerce and trade – not just by consulting their lists but perhaps by belonging to them or addressing their meetings;
❑ public libraries – particularly as a source of some of the items mentioned later in this list;
❑ his suppliers – among the companies he buys from, such as office equipment and supplies firms, some may be potential customers;
❑ credit bureaux or other professional service agents;
❑ personal observation – the factory down the road, the new office block on the corner;
❑ local government offices;
❑ referrals – existing customers, suppliers' customers, contacts or friends;
❑ his bank;
❑ mailing lists – often available for rent as well as from directories;
❑ exhibitions and trade promotion events;
❑ local hotels – which already receive business from him and may be helpful in return. (What meetings or exhibitions go on there?);
❑ company annual reports (from his public library);
❑ company house/employee magazines (from his public library);
❑ trade/industry/technical journals (from his public library);
❑ directories of companies (from his public library);
❑ telephone directories/Yellow Pages (from his public library).

One or a combination of these can supply valuable information about prospects: the names of companies, what business they are in and if it is going well or badly, whether they export, how big they are, who owns them, what subsidiaries or associates they have and, last but not least, who runs and manages them.

Exactly which individual is then approached is vital, and may not be a simple decision. Indeed, it may be that several people are involved, for example those who travel, those who send them, those who pay and, perhaps, those who make the bookings. Many secretaries have considerable discretionary power in making company travel bookings, and not least among their considerations will be how straightforward and easy their dealings with the travel agency are.

As well as considering which individual to approach, an important assessment at this stage is that of financial potential. How much business might be obtained from the company in, say, a year? This analysis will rule out some prospects as not being worth further pursuit. Experience will sharpen the accuracy with which these decisions can be made, but meanwhile a good first list should be developing.

The old military maxim that 'time spent in reconnaissance is seldom wasted' is a good one. In war it can help to prevent casualties. In business it not only produces information, in this case on who should be contacted, but it also provides a platform for a more accurately conceived, more successful approach.

Having identified who will be contacted, the next step is organizing the approach. A number of factors may be important here, both before an approach is made and in the follow-up. There are two key areas our manager needs to consider before making an approach:

Selecting the method of approach

The ultimate objective is almost certainly a face-to-face meeting, which must be held before any substantial business can result. Such a meeting can be set up by:

❑ 'cold calling' (calling without an appointment);
❑ sending a letter or card with or without supporting literature;
❑ telephoning 'cold' or as follow-up to a letter or promotion;

❏ getting people together, initially as a group, and making a presentation at your premises, a hotel or other venue, or through a third party (such as at a chamber of trade meeting).

The logistics are also important. What is needed is a campaign spread over time so that, if and when favourable responses occur, they can be followed up promptly; such responses may be more difficult to cope with if they all occur together.

Deciding who will take the action

The process will almost certainly involve approaching, meeting and discussing matters with people senior in, and knowledgeable about, their own business. The approach therefore needs to be made by people with the right profile, who will be perceived as being appropriate, and who can really give an impression of competence. They also need to have the right attitude, wanting to win business in what may be a new and perhaps more difficult area. They need the knowledge and skills to tackle the task in hand: knowledge of the customers, the agency and its. services, of overseas places, and processes, or the ability to find out quickly.

Detail is important. The export manager who is made late for an appointment will be equally upset by missing a flight connection or simply by being misinformed on the time it takes to get from airport to hotel. The travel agent, rightly or wrongly, will probably get the blame.

Finally, skills in customer contact, selling and negotiation are needed, as well as skills in all the areas, such as writing sales letters, involved in making the approach. Making the right choice of person is therefore crucial and, in the long term, a small company set on developing its business travel side may need to consider recruitment, training or both.

The initial approach is vital, as with any first impression, and it may be very difficult, after an initial negative response, to organize a second chance. Having thought the process through in this way, the chances of success are that much greater.

However it is set up, once contact occurs the salesperson has to carry it through and, to do this, must understand the potential buyers and make the contact with them both persuasive and acceptable; in other words, the contact must not be so 'pushy' as to be self-defeating.

THE SALES PROCESS

Selling goes through various stages. Here we begin to review what must take place. It starts, as was said above, with an understanding of the buyer. No one can sell effectively without understanding how people make decisions to purchase. A good way of thinking about it, one originated by psychologists in the United States, suggests that the buyer's decision-making goes through seven distinct stages, as follows:

❑ I am important and I want to be respected.
❑ Consider my needs.
❑ How will your ideas help me?
❑ What are the facts?
❑ What are the snags?
❑ What shall I do?
❑ I approve.

It helps explain this if you consider what you do if faced with a decision to purchase, say, a new refrigerator. You want to deal with someone who is not only polite but also concerned for you as a customer, and who is prepared to discover and take on board your needs (what size is necessary to fit the kitchen, or what is your view of economy or price). You want someone whose suggestions helpfully adhere to the brief, who gives you sufficient information on which to base a decision and who is able to handle your queries without becoming defensive or argumentative. Not least, you want someone who explains, and makes clear and straightforward, any administrative points (delivery, payment terms, etc), allowing you to weigh things up and make a decision in the confidence that you will be pleased with your choice.

Customers must do what they feel is necessary; indeed the way selling is conducted must allow this to happen. The two keys to success – 'closing the sale', as obtaining a buying commitment is called – are the process of matching the buyer's progression through the decision-making process, and describing, selectively, the product, discussing it in a way that relates to precisely what a (particular) buyer needs.

Early on, because customers need to go through other stages, the salesperson may not always be able to aim for a commitment to buy, but must have a clear objective on which to close. This may be to get customers to allow literature to be sent to them, to fix an appointment to meet or to provide sufficient information for a detailed quotation to be prepared. Whatever objective is set, however, it is important to know and be able to recognize the various stages ahead. With any customer contact (by telephone or letter, as well as face to face), the salesperson must monitor customer progress and respond flexibly and appropriately to accommodate it.

The whole buying process is not always covered in only one contact between the company and the customer. Every initial contact does not result in a sale, and neither does it result in a lost sale. Some stages of the selling sequence have to be followed up in each sales contact, but the logic applies equally to a series of calls forming the whole sales approach. For doubtful customers, or sales of great complexity and expense, there may be numerous contacts to cover just one of the stages before buyers are satisfied and can move on to the next stage. Each call or contact has a selling sequence of its own in reaching the call objectives. Each call is a part of an overall selling sequence aimed at reaching overall sales objectives.

Planning the selling sequence is therefore as much a part of call planning as it is of sales planning, but only rarely does a call take place exactly as planned. Knowing and using the sales sequence and being able to recognize stages of the buying process are, however, invaluable if salespeople are to realize their potential for direct sales results.

With this basic appreciation of buyers and what directs their reactions, we can look more closely at the key areas of the sales approach.

PUTTING OVER PRODUCT INFORMATION PERSUASIVELY

Identifying with buyers, in order to recognize the stages of the buying process and to match them with a parallel selling sequence, must extend to the presentation of the sales proposition. Nowhere is this more important than in the way salespeople look at the product or service that they are selling.

Product knowledge is too often taken for granted by companies and salespeople. Sadly, experience of hearing hundreds of salespeople talking unintelligible gibberish does not support this complacency. Salespeople are too often given inadequate product knowledge and what is given is slanted towards the company, not the customer. Managers are often still heard to say proudly, 'Everyone joining us spends six months in the factory, to learn the business', but many then emerge with no better idea of what the product means *to the customer*. Everyone with any role to play in sales-oriented customer contact must consider the product, and all that goes with it, from the customer's point of view.

HOW BENEFITS HELP SELLING

If salespeople get into the habit of seeing things through customers' eyes, they will realize that they do not sell special promotions; free trial-offers or fancy wrappings do not really sell products either. Salespeople sell what customers want to buy – not products or services in themselves, but benefits.

What are benefits? This concept is key to successful selling and deserves a clear definition. Benefits are what products, promotions or services *do for or mean to* customers. For example, people do not buy electric drills because they want electric drills, but because they want to be able to make holes. They buy holes, not drills. They buy drills for what they will do (make holes). This in turn may only be important to them because of a need for storage and a requirement to put up shelving.

When this is realized, selling becomes more effective and also easier. Salespeople do not have to try to sell the same product to a lot of different people, but meet each person's needs with personal benefits. Benefits are what things sold can do for individual customers. Different customers buy the same product for different reasons. Therefore, you must identify and use the particular benefits of interest to them. What a product *is* is represented by its features. What a product *does* is described by its benefits. If salespeople forget this, then the things that are important to customers will not always be seen as important from the seller's viewpoint, particularly if he or she has had little or no sales training. The result can, understandably, end up in a conflict of priorities, with salespeople concentrating on what is important to them (their company, product and the need to sell), while customers unsurprisingly take their own view, one that reflects their priorities and needs.

Customers are most unlikely to see things from the selling point of view. Everyone is to him or herself the most important person in the world. Therefore, to be successful, sellers have to see things from the customer point of view and demonstrate through words and actions that they have done so. Their chances of success are greater if they can understand the needs of the people they talk to and make them realize that they (the sellers) can help them fulfil their needs.

Doing this necessitates the correct use of benefits. In presenting any proposition to customers, even simply recommending a product in reply to a query, salespeople should always translate what they are offering into what it will do. A company, and the people who write its sales literature, may grow product-orientated, and gradual product development can reinforce this attitude by adding more and more features. It is only a small step before everyone is busy trying to sell the product on its features alone. It is interesting to note that often, when this happens, advertising and selling become more and more forceful, with the features being given a frantic push, as passing time reveals that there has been no great rush to buy.

Two familiar examples are the audio and camera markets. Stereo equipment, in particular, is almost always promoted on features only. Masses of technical terms, most of them meaningless to the majority of end users, dominate advertisements and brochures, while the visual communication is based entirely on the appearance of the amplifier, speakers and other 'boxes'. Yet what people want from a stereo set is sound and reliability – years of listening pleasure. Cameras are often sold on the same features-orientated basis.

When competitive products become almost identical in their performance, it can be difficult to sell benefits, since all options seem to offer the same benefits. Choice then often depends on the personal appeal of some secondary feature. But even then, there must be emphasis on the benefits of those features, rather than on the features themselves. In industrial selling (to other companies rather than to individual consumers), it is more important than ever to concentrate on benefits rather than on features that may be little better than gimmicks. Features are only important if they support benefits that the customer is interested in.

Deciding to concentrate on benefits is only half the battle, however. They have to be the right benefits. In fact, benefits are only important to customers if they describe the satisfaction of the customers' needs. Working out the needs, and then the benefits, means that all salespeople must put themselves in the customers' shoes.

SPECIFIC APPROACHES FOR INDIVIDUAL CUSTOMERS

To know what benefits to put forward, salespeople must know what customers' needs are; and to know those needs, they have to know exactly who the customers are. Very often, customers are also those who actually use the product. Frequently, however, direct customers are purchasers or decision-makers, but not users. This is most common in industrial selling, when a buying department may be responsible for ordering, as well as handling the purchasing of, most of a company's requirements. In consumer products, a manufacturer may sell to a wholesaler, the wholesaler to a retailer, and it is only the retailer that actually sells to users.

The requirements of the end user are also of interest to the various intermediaries, but the best results will be obtained if salespeople bear in mind the needs of both buyers and users, and the differences between their various needs.

Note that not all needs are objective. Most buyers, including industrial ones, also have subjective requirements, which are reflected in their decisions. No product is bought on an entirely objective or subjective basis. Sometimes, even with technical products, once all the objective needs have been met, the final decision can be heavily influenced by subjective factors, perhaps seemingly of minor significance. For example, someone buying hotel facilities for a conference may be as concerned about the atmosphere of a venue as about measurable factors such as whether the group will physically fit in a meeting room.

Matching benefits to individual customer needs makes a sale more likely, for a product's benefits must match a buyer's needs. The features are only what give a product the right benefits. By going through this process for particular products, and for segments of the range, and matching the factors identified to customer needs, a complete 'databank' of product information from the customer viewpoint can be organized.

With competitive products becoming increasingly similar, more buyers quickly conclude that their main needs can be met by more than one product. Other needs then become more important. If, for instance, a buyer needs a crane, there will probably be a number of options, all of which lift the weight required, and cost practically the same. The deciding factors then become availability, service, repair facilities and so on. Sellers can look at the 'features' contained by the company as a whole and be ready to convert them to benefits to customers, in the same way that they can practise finding benefits for the full product range.

Every aspect of the company and its offering can, potentially, be described in terms of benefits. They include aspects arising from the products (price, packaging, design, etc), allied services (after-sales service, credit, etc), the company itself (size, reputation, etc), and the people involved (their knowledge, skill and character).

Each such item could be a source of benefit to potential customers and, as they recognize this, they move closer to becoming actual customers. By 'thinking benefits' and by seeing things from the customers' point of view, salespeople can make a real contribution to sales and company profitability.

THE DANGERS OF UNRESTRAINED JARGON

A final hazard, which can destroy the customer orientation of sales contacts, is jargon. 'Professional slang' comes in two main forms, both of which can confuse customers.

Technical or industrial jargon

Salespeople should always let customers be first to use it. Technological complexities have already led to thousands of new words and phrases in business and industry, and introducing still more new terms seldom helps. But worst of all is the possibility that customers will not know what is being talked about, or will form the wrong impression, yet hesitate to admit it.

Organization jargon

It is even more important to avoid the internal jargon of a particular organization, for here the customer will be on very unfamiliar ground. There is a world of difference between someone saying, 'We'll do a sales/stock return compo and let you know shortly' and, 'To answer your query, we'll have to do a comparison of the sales and stock return movements. The quickest way will be to ask for a computer printout, which Head Office will forward to us. I will contact you with the answer in a week or 10 days' time'.

Company jargon can have a wide effect, not only when used in selling, and even simple phrases can cause trouble. Delivery is one area for potential misunderstanding. Promising 'immediate delivery' might mean getting the product to the customer within a week, when normal delivery takes three weeks. But what if the customer is in the pharmaceutical industry, where 'immediate delivery' is jargon for 'within eight hours'? He or she is almost bound to get the wrong impression.

FINDING OUT

However, saying the right things is not all there is to selling. A critical stage is asking the right questions and listening – *really listening* – to the answers, using these answers as a guide to how to proceed.

Knowing how and why customers buy is a prerequisite to successful selling and, because all customers are individuals and want to be treated as such, selling must be based on finding out exactly what each customer wants, and why. In other words, questioning (and listening to and using the answers) is as important to selling as simply presenting the case.

It is important to start asking questions early in the approach, and asking the right questions in the right way is crucial. Two kinds of question are important in getting it right:

1. *Open questions*: those that cannot be answered by 'yes' or 'no', but get the customer talking. These work best and produce the most useful information.
2. *Probing questions*: those that go beyond enquiring about the background situation, to exploring problems and implications and identifying real needs.

HOW IT WORKS

We can illustrate these techniques by quoting a possible conversation between the travel agent referred to earlier and one of his prospects.

Agent: What areas are currently your priority, Mr Export Manager?

Prospect: The Middle East is top priority for investigation, but short term, Germany has been more important.

Agent: What makes that so?

Prospect: Well, we're exhibiting at a trade fair in Germany. This will tie up a number of staff and eat up a lot of the budget. Our exploratory visit to the Middle East may have to wait.

Agent: Won't that cause problems, seeing as you had intended to go earlier?

Prospect: I suppose it will. With the lead times involved it may rule out the chances of tying up any deals for this financial year.

Agent: Had you thought of moving one of your people straight on from Germany to the Middle East, Mr Export Manager?

Prospect: Er, no.

Agent: I think I could show some real savings over making two separate trips. If you did it this way, the lead time wouldn't slip. Would that be of interest?

Prospect: Could be. If I give you some dates, can we map something out to show exactly how it could be done?

Agent: Certainly . . .

This kind of questioning not only produces information, but can be used creatively to spot opportunities. It accurately pinpoints the prospect's real needs and allows an accurate response to them. Most prospects not only like talking about their own situation but also react favourably to this approach. They may well see the genuine identification of their problems, and the offer of solutions to them, as distinctly different from a competitive approach that simply catalogues the product or services offered.

In this case, it also allows much better demonstration of two benefits that purchasers look for from travel agents: objectivity and expertise. The more these are apparent, the more the agency is differentiated from the competition.

THE PROFESSIONAL SALES APPROACH

So far this section has concentrated on certain factors inherent in the sales job, particularly those that demand, like everything in marketing, a customer orientation and may be relevant to others in the company; these include finding out customer needs and emphasizing benefits.

Of course, there is more to it than that. In a short book able to give only limited space to each of its topics, perhaps it is sensible to suggest that, for those wanting more detail, further reading would be useful. (For example, *101 Ways to Increase Sales* (Forsyth, 1996, also from Kogan Page) provides a useful reference for anyone who wants a complete rundown on the selling job.) So, with the proviso that we are dealing only with key issues, let us mention just a few more factors.

First, there are some basics. To be successful, field sales staff must be able to:

❑ *plan*: they must see the right people, and the right number of people, regularly if necessary;
❑ *prepare*: sales contact needs thinking through. The so-called 'born sales person' is very rare. The best of the rest do – and benefit from – their homework;
❑ *understand the customer*: they should use empathy (the ability to put themselves in the 'customer's shoes'), base what they do on real needs, and talk benefits;
❑ *project the appropriate manner*: not all salespeople are welcome, and not all can position themselves as advisors or whatever makes their approach acceptable – being accepted needs working at;
❑ *conduct a good meeting*: they must stay in control and direct the contact, yet make customers think they are getting what they want;
❑ *listen*: this is a much undervalued skill in selling;
❑ *handle objections*: the pros and cons need debating – selling is not about winning arguments or scoring points

❏ *be persistent*: this means asking for a commitment and, if necessary, asking again.

Secondly, a variety of additional skills may be necessary to operate professionally in a sales role. These include:

❏ account analysis and planning;
❏ the writing skills necessary for proposal/quotation documents that are as persuasive as face-to-face contact;
❏ skills of formal presentation;
❏ numeracy and negotiation skills.

And all this is required from a job in which people are said to be 'only in sales'.

There is an old saying that 'selling starts when the customer says yes', meaning that any company wanting long-term, repeat business must work at it, ensuring that the ongoing sales process continues to act to retain and develop business for the future. Again, the principles can be illustrated by reference to the travel agency manager.

The manager knows that in winning more business travel the overall objective is not one order, but ongoing profitable business from this area. Whether customers are retained, buy again and buy more is dependent primarily on two factors:

1. *Service*: It almost goes without saying, but promises of service must be fulfilled to the letter; if they are not, the customer will notice. A number of different people may be involved in servicing the account. They all have to appreciate its importance and get their bit right. If the customer was promised information by 3.30 pm, a visa by the end of the week, two suggested itineraries in writing and a reservation in a certain hotel at a particular price, then he or she should get just that. Even minor variations, such as information by 4 pm and a slight price difference on room rate, do matter. Promise what can be done – and do it 100 per cent.

2. *Follow-up*: Even if the service received is first class, the manager must continue to sell to the customer after the order as follows:
   - Check with him or her after the trip.
   - Check who else is involved in the next purchase – the customer's secretary, or other managers?
   - Ask more questions. When is the next trip? When should contact be made again?
   - Make suggestions. Can booking be made earlier? Would the customer like to take his or her partner on the next trip?
   - Anticipate. Does the customer know fares are going up? Can the trip be made earlier to save money?
   - Explore what else the customer might buy.
   - Investigate who else in the company travels – other staff, departments, subsidiaries?
   - See whether holiday information can be distributed in the company.
   - Write to the customer. Do not let him or her forget you. Make sure you are thought of first.

A positive follow-up programme of this sort can certainly potentially make marketing work better. It can maximize the chances of repeat business and ensure that opportunities to sell additional products or services are not missed. Such an approach brings us full circle, from identifying and contacting prospects for the first time, to holding and developing their business on a continuing basis. .

Selling – certainly effective selling – does not just happen. The management process that is responsible for it is important.

SALES MANAGEMENT

It is not enough for a company simply to push salespeople out into the field and say, 'Sell'. As with other people, salespeople need managing; why else have sales managers, as most organizations of any size do? Usually such managers are very much part of the overall management and marketing team. In small companies, they may have many tasks and responsibilities that are really general management functions. In addition, the people managing sales teams usually handle a certain number of customers, usually larger ones, personally.

There is nothing wrong with this, and indeed such involvement is useful, but it can dilute the time available for the classic sales management functions and this, in turn, can leave sales less effective. In industries where suitable time is put into managing sales teams, the investment it represents is regarded as both necessary and worth while. Most usually, the classic tasks of sales management are regarded as falling into six areas, which are:

1. *Planning*: Time needs to be spent planning the scope and extent of the sales operation, its budget and what it aims to achieve. Achievement is organized first around targets and setting targets, not just for the amount to be sold, but also for profitability, product mix, etc, and is a key task. If the product range is large, then this makes it especially important that the team's activities are directed with the right focus.
2. *Organization*: The number of salespeople required needs to be calculated (it is not just a matter of what can be afforded, but of customer service and coverage, though the two go together), as does how and where they are deployed. The question of the various market sectors involved must be addressed, looking not just at who calls on customers in, say, Hertfordshire, but at how major accounts are dealt with and the strategy for any non-traditional outlets, which may well need separate consideration. Organizations selling to groups of customers that differ radically from one another may separate the different sales tasks, and even have separate sales teams.
3. *Staffing*: This is vital; it is no good, as the saying goes, 'paying peanuts and employing monkeys'. If the sales resource is to be effective, then it must be recognized that recruitment and selection need a professional approach, and the best possible team must be appointed. The job is to represent the firm, to differentiate it from the competition and to sell effectively – certainly and continuously. Recruitment may be a chore, but

selecting the best of a poor bunch (rather than re-advertising and starting the whole thing over again) should simply not be an option. It is evident from even a cursory scan of typical job advertisements how much emphasis is put on past experience in many industries. As people tend to be sought at a youngish age (when they are cheaper?), maybe more fresh blood might sometimes be usefully contemplated. The experience route is fine, but one effect can be to encourage the duds to circulate around a particular industry. If people only do an average job for one company, what makes it likely that they will suddenly do better for another?

4. *Development*: This is an ongoing process. Because there is no one 'right' way to sell, what is necessary is to deploy the appropriate approach literally day by day, meeting by meeting, customer by customer, and continue to fine-tune both the approaches and the skills that generate them over the long term. If the team is to be professional in this sense, then more than a brief induction is necessary; an ongoing continuum of field development is necessary.

5. *Motivation*: Like development, motivation does not just happen (this is true of so much in management), but it needs time, effort and consideration. Salespeople spend a great deal of time on their own, and are exposed to the attrition of the attitude that can come from customers who are not exactly 'on their side'. As a group, they need considerable motivation. Like training, motivation is not simply a 'good thing' but increases sales and makes performance more certain. Sales management must work at this area systematically. It affects overall issues such as pay and other rewards (for example, any commission scheme must act as a real incentive – not simply reward past performance – and therefore must be well conceived and arranged). Motivation also affects many smaller issues. Just saying 'well done' is an element of motivation, but how many managers, whatever their role, can put their hands on their heart and swear they have found time to do even that sufficiently often in, say, the last month? There is so much involved here – communications, effective sales meetings

and good organization. For example, letting salespeople act without good support material to show may well make selling more difficult and thus be demotivational. This is especially so if those struggling to do it feel that it has only been made necessary by inefficiency somewhere in the organization. Motivation has a broad remit and involves a wider group of people than sales managers alone.

6. *Control*: Constant monitoring is necessary if the team is to remain on track and thus hit targets. Action must be taken to anticipate and correct any shortfall, and this is traditionally the role of control. It is at least as important, however, to monitor *positive* variances. If something is going better than plan, then it needs to be asked why – maybe there are lessons to be learnt from the answer that can help repeat the good performance or spread the effect more widely.

It is simply not possible to run a truly effective team without spending sufficient time with individuals in the field, using accompanied calls first to observe and evaluate, and then to counsel and fine-tune performance. Without this, performance can never be maximized, and indeed a whole area of activity will go by default. Although results show what is being achieved, figures alone cannot, by definition, show *how* things are being done in the field and whether performance could benefit from fine-tuning. Only by direct involvement can sales managers put themselves in a position to know what action might improve performance, and take it. Many regard this as the single most important aspect of the sales management job. The reason is entirely practical: time spent on it acts to increase sales. Not least, the process is valuable in ensuring that salespeople adopt a practical and constructive approach to what they can do day to day to refine their own techniques and improve performance. Whatever the support given by sales management, salespeople themselves are, after all, the only coaches who are there all the time.

All in all, sales management has a wide and vital brief. The quality of sales management is often readily discernible from the state of the sales team. Excellence in sales management makes a real difference. Time spent on all aspects of sales management can have direct influence on sales results.

SALES PRODUCTIVITY

One further area is worth mentioning. Whatever quality is brought to sales calls, sales results are influenced by more than this. The other crucial factors are:

❑ who is seen (the selection of appropriate prospects/buyers/ customers);
❑ how many people are seen;
❑ how often they are seen (the call frequency decided upon and how it varies and is used).

If these productivity factors are well organized, and worked at on a regular basis, then the overall results are likely to be improved. It is a differentiating factor between the good and less good salespeople in any industry, and applies, albeit in slightly different ways, to all categories of customer, depending on the nature of the business.

Productivity comes first from seeing the right people, and having the right outlets. It also means seeing the right individuals throughout larger outlets, where salespeople may have to see several people in different departments (as in selling, say, training services to a company where purchase might be made by personnel, training or functional departments).

Secondly, productivity comes from sheer quantity. Providing call quality is not sacrificed, then the more people seen, the more products or services sold. Thirdly, there is the question of frequency. The rule here is often stated as to call the *minimum* number of times that will preserve and build the business. Some accounts are called on every week. Others may be seen only once a year. Everyone, and this may affect smaller companies especially, must consider frequency very carefully. Sometimes purely personal factors influence this sort of productivity. On a wet Friday afternoon in a British February, many salespeople may be tempted to go for a convenient call mid-afternoon – one which is *en route* for home and where they are likely to get a reasonable welcome and a nice cup of tea! – rather than maximize productivity.

What is the frequency that will create some sort of continuity? How quickly do memories fade? What about the industry cycle, buying cycle, seasonality or financial year? Many factors may need to be considered in making a judgement. These factors and more are all important – as are the economics involved – but customer service is always important, and if frequency falls below a certain level any real continuity becomes difficult if not impossible to create.

This is an area for considered action, not an unthinking reiteration of the existing pattern. The detail here makes a difference, and it is worth spending time in analysis and planning to get it right. Overall, selling is a key area and one where regular and suitable thought can help make it work better; indeed it is another area that demands constant fine-tuning in a dynamic marketplace.

8

CUSTOMER CARE

Looking after customers is inherent to better marketing. Customer service, as customers both anticipate and experience it, is fundamental to success. It is not overstating it to suggest it is a basic foundation, which underpins ongoing overall marketing success. The whole process is nowadays most often called 'customer care', and its careful execution – in a way designed to impress customers – provides a significant opportunity to differentiate an organization from its competitors.

EXCELLENCE IN CUSTOMER CARE

It has already been mentioned that it is increasingly difficult for customers to differentiate between many of the competing products and services in the market. In many industries, products are essentially similar in terms of design, performance and specification, at least within a given price bracket. This is as true of industrial products as of consumer goods. Often customers' final choices will, therefore, be influenced as much by subjective areas as anything else. The nature of customer service can play a major role in this, sometimes becoming the most important factor.

The precise nature and manner of customer service adopted becomes an integral part of producing an organization's image. Indeed, customer service should both reflect any existing image and extend it. For example, if a company wants to be seen as efficient, modern, innovative or whatever, then its customer service must reflect such qualities. A company positioning itself as caring or advisory (in healthcare or financial services, for example) cannot skimp the time spent with customers without being thought deficient. Even little things can dilute an image. Consider something as simple as the effect of a direct mailshot, or simple sales letter. It may do a good job, sound right, prompt interest and commend urgency, but be let down by the fact that the reply-paid envelope enclosed with it is second class (something that in the UK can routinely take four or more days to arrive). Even choosing such a simple example makes a point; the greater damage of worse mistakes is obvious.

Conversely, good customer care practice can have specific positive effect. Again consider a simple case. In the (training) business of one of the authors of this book, the source of ring binders used for the many courses and seminars conducted was, for a while, influenced almost exclusively – in a commodity-type product area with many suppliers offering similar products – by the efficiency and customer orientation of one person in the supplier's sales office. When she left them, the business was subsequently moved elsewhere. The antithesis of this is the 'abominable "no" man' who too often seems to inhabit the sales office, and who can destroy months of work by management and sales staff, miss opportunities and lose orders, or indeed customers, in a moment, maybe in one brief telephone call. Everyone has his or her favourite horror story, which may say something about prevailing standards.

THE OPPORTUNITY OF PREVAILING STANDARDS

Any shortfall in prevailing standards presents an opportunity for others in the industry to steal an edge by getting it right; this opportunity is surely not so difficult to take advantage of and use to create a better position in the market.

It is not a question of aiming for some idea of perfection (after all, both McDonalds restaurants and the Ritz Hotel claim to offer good service, but in very different ways – and they are both right to say so), but any company must organize things positively to achieve the standards they have decided they – or rather their customers – require.

What creates good customer care? It comes primarily through the careful consideration of both staffing and organization. It is not easy. The mix of characteristics and considerations that can help make success more likely is not easy to define; what we can be sure of is that customers know all too readily what they like – and the reverse – when they encounter it. One time when such a judgement is made is when a complaint is being handled. We will get this negative instance out of the way first, before considering the positive aspects of customer contact.

HANDLING COMPLAINTS

The first task is to reduce the number of complaints that must be dealt with. Every organization doubtless gets some, but everything that can give rise to them – the product or service, customer service and such factors as delivery, policy and people – must be examined to ensure that no complaints are occurring (especially with something happening repeatedly) that could be avoided.

Complaints are a source of feedback and intelligence. The job is not simply to field them and forget them. It is to learn from them, and use what is learnt to make things better for the future. Simple feedback and reporting systems may be necessary – collecting, centralizing and analysing data – so that positive action to improve things can be taken.

Complaints must be handled in the right way. Complaint handling is not an argument. The usual human reaction of some-one left not briefed is to be defensive – 'it's not my fault'. That may well be, but the job of the complaint handler is to sort out the problem and win back the customer, not to save face. Speaking for the organization, taking the blame if necessary, and doing so in a positive manner however he or she may feel goes with the territory. Things must be sorted out but, beyond that, it is *how* it is done that can reinforce the image.

Much is lost by organizations that allow complaints to be 'fought off'; the best policy is almost always to meet them head on:

❑ Say sorry.
❑ Take appropriate action.
❑ Do so without making customers feel bad.
❑ Exceed their expectations of good service.
❑ Follow up if appropriate (eg with a letter of apology).
❑ Apologize again.

Long convoluted arguments, designed to save the organization a small amount of money, are almost always negated by added time as customers dig in their heels – 'they will not get away with this' – and settle down to a long exchange of correspondence. For example . . . but we digress. We all have favourite stories in this area, and that too perhaps makes a point. Giving people the benefit of the doubt is usually the best policy (though remember, there are some professional complainers whom perhaps you should stand up to).

It is said that if something is really well done customers may tell someone about it – more than one if it really makes a mark. But if something is done badly, they will tell 10 times that number about it. There is no contest over which is better.

POSITIVE CONTACT

There are a number of ways in which communication occurs between an organization and its customers. Each presents different problems and opportunities and is worth examining separately, though it should always be borne in mind that what ultimately creates customer satisfaction, or the reverse, is the cumulative effect of a variety of ongoing contacts where this is what occurs.

Telephone contact

This is a very particular kind of contact. Obviously, it is voice only. This means that what is said and how it is said must come over just right. Some things cannot be described in words alone – try describing how to tie a shoelace, for example – but if a customer has been sent something, then the conversation is very different if both parties look at it together.

Many telephone conversations take place with the company employee at a computer screen. It must be remembered that customers cannot see the screen. A pause while something is being entered or summoned up on screen may be read as impolite by a customer unaware of what is being done. Explanation along the way is vital, as is an appropriate manner and all the usual courtesies – from a prompt answer to use of the customer's name.

Written contact

Putting things in writing seems to be a problem for many. It is often a weak area, as the many dreary or gobbledegook-type documents circulating around and between organizations bear testimony to. Those involved in it – whether they are writing a simple sales letter or a more complex document such as a proposal – should acquire the necessary skills to execute it well (see *How to be Better at Writing Reports and Proposals* (Forsyth, 1997) in this series).

Every different methodology is worth individual thought to ensure it is handled appropriately. Is a letter right, or a fax (with its suggestion of urgency) or an e-mail? Letters can look good, faxes do not reproduce your smart letterhead and may fade away over time, and an e-mail can be deleted in a split second at the touch of a button. All these factors and more need balancing before taking action, and the outcome must match method with intention. Sometimes the answer is a combination, for example an urgent message sent quickly by e-mail and confirmed in smarter form by letter. Just because prevailing standards tend to be poor (and it may be worth while to get hold of items that your competitors send out for comparison), there is a significant opportunity to create better customer reactions than your competitors do.

Face-to-face contact

Members of the field sales team may have face-to-face contact, as may those in many other circumstances such as in a showroom, at an exhibition or trade show or in a retail situation. Unlike telephone communication, everything that goes on in face-to-face contact is important, from a friendly smile (or look of serious consideration, if that is more suitable) to body language. (It is easy for the embarrassment of an uncertain new member of staff to come over as indifference or even arrogance.)

Each method involves its own particular characteristics and may demand different skills. This is not the place to review the considerable detail of all the skills involved, though it is worth noting that it may need investigation by whoever is to carry out the contacts. It is, however, worth summarizing certain key issues that are common to all customer contact, both because this is useful in its own right and because it exemplifies the need for attention to detail across the whole area of customer care.

WHAT CUSTOMERS WANT

To summarize succinctly we will use a mnemonic much favoured by trainers. It states that customer contact should be PERFECT. The letters stand for:

❑ *Polite*: This almost goes without saying. Politeness should be manifest throughout the process of communication with customers. It must be genuine – grovelling will reverse the desired effect – and a pleasant personal touch will enhance it. It must be maintained whatever the circumstances and the pressures.

❏ *Efficient*: Things have got to be done right, and that means for customers' convenience rather than to fit in with an organization's systems, particularly bureaucratic ones.

❏ *Respectful*: This is important and must match the customer. Some want respect much in evidence, and others less so, but it must always be there. (An understanding of customer attitude to time is a good example: do customers want everything done in a moment because they are in a hurry, or do they see time spent on something as evidence of thoroughness or care?)

❏ *Friendly*: The level of friendliness must be judged just right. Not every customer wants too much of it too soon, but everyone wants the transaction to be pleasant.

❏ *Enthusiastic*: Interest in the customer – something most regard as a prerequisite for good customer care – is suggested by enthusiasm.

❏ *Cheerful*: This must be maintained even in the face of adversity. Customers do not want to feel that the whole business of their being dealt with is getting someone down.

❏ *Tactful*: Many customer situations have aspects that are confidential or sensitive, and respect for such aspects is appreciated.

Overall the above sums up the style of handling that works best; the final trick is to apply it individually. Customers like to be dealt with as individuals for the very good reason that that is what they are. Anything that smacks of a standard approach – dealing with them on 'automatic pilot' – dilutes the good that customer contact can do. There are plenty of opportunities to make customer contact better that the competition's, and to gain from the process.

MANAGING TO PRODUCE GOOD CUSTOMER CARE

Excellence of customer care does not just happen. Managers must manage the process and the people involved. Those who do so have a job that involves a number of different elements. Thus:

❑ it is not enough for the managers responsible for support areas only to be good administrators, although without the sorting out of priorities and smooth handling of enquiries, files, paperwork, correspondence and records, sales support will never be effective;

❑ it is not enough for them only to be good salespeople, although it is essential that they have an understanding of or familiarity with sales techniques, that they are able to recognize sales opportunities, and that they ensure both they and members of their team take those opportunities;

❑ it is not enough for them only to be effective managers of people, although it is vital that they are able to lead and motivate a close-knit and enthusiastic team, tackling a diverse range of activity in hectic conditions.

Managers also have to understand and pass on an understanding of the role of sales support, so that all concerned see it as a vital tactical weapon in the overall marketing operation. This means that they must have an appreciation of what marketing is and the various ways in which, directly or indirectly, the sales office and sales support or customer care staff can contribute to company profitability.

This implies a knowledge of, and involvement in, the marketing process. For example, if sales support personnel are not told (or do not ask) about the relative profitability of different products, they may be busy pushing product A when product B, similar in price or even more expensive, makes more money.

FOCUS ON PRIORITIES

A prerequisite for contributing effectively for any manager is to be able to identify priorities. With a variety of activities, and with incoming calls and enquiries being unpredictable, managers either adhere to rigid sets of rules that allow things to be coped with and run an adequate office, or have the skill and initiative to recognize different priorities and get the best out of them, so building up a really effective operation.

Identifying priorities is of little use, however, unless managers are able to organize to deal with them. This calls for abilities in managing and controlling time, systems and people. To be effective, they must be consistent sales-oriented managers of people, able to accept ideas from others, cope with the problems of the urgent and balance this with the opportunities of the important. There is an important link with the various electronic systems used in customer service. It is not untypical for a company to be able to call up customers' full details on a computer screen instantly, just by tapping in their account number or postcode. Systems must be organized in every way that facilitates customer service (yet how often do complaining customers hear systems – and policy – blamed for the inability to give proper customer service?).

The sales support team must be organized to produce an ongoing positive cycle of repeat business from its contacts. Even negative contacts such as complaints can be dealt with as part of a positive cycle involving a range of possible contacts with the customer, either directly or through other sections of the company. Although possibly low among company priorities, sales support in fact occupies a central position, which is vital in terms of contacts and influence.

There is a requirement for close and constructive co-operation with other sections of the company, for example production, or the sales force. Poor liaison can cause problems. In one company, for instance, sales office staff spent time handling complaints about delivery on 75 per cent of orders that went through, not because delivery was bad, but because the sales force was quoting six weeks delivery when everyone in the company knew it was normally eight weeks. Such unnecessarily wasted time could have been used more constructively to increase sales.

There are, of course, exceptions, but prevailing standards of sales office service, and the selling that is inextricably bound up with them, are often not high, or not as high as they could be. It should not be difficult, therefore, not only to make customer contact stand out in a way that really impresses customers, but also genuinely to increase sales results. For many firms, this is a real opportunity area that is too often neglected.

There are no excuses for not selling. Time pressure, work pressure, staffing, equipment and resources may all make it more difficult, but what ensures real selling does take place is first, attitude and second, skills and knowledge of how to do it effectively. Only management can get this over and maintain standards. It is, in fact, much easier to run a 'tight ship', and to set standards and stick to them, than to let things go by default. People are motivated by belonging to the 'best team' and come to care about standards and performance very much.

Selling must not be confused with simple customer service, however efficient and courteous – which is not to deny the vital importance of service and courteousness. Selling forms one of the bases for success, as does product knowledge – not just knowing about the product, but being able to talk about it in such a way as to make sense to the customer. This does not just happen. Management must ensure that it happens. The same applies to sales technique. The sales office team (all of them with customer contact) must have a basic knowledge of the sales process, augmented by knowledge of and ability to apply particular skills, on the telephone or in letter-writing, for instance, and backed as necessary by sheer persistence and inventiveness. We have concentrated here on service and its role in linking with and assisting sales; other aspects of selling were covered in Chapter 7.

As stated before, none of this just happens. Management is responsible for recruiting the right people, for their initial training and ongoing development, and for motivating them on a continuing basis. As with so many topics reviewed here, customer service and the internal sales effort have more to them than meets the eye. Think about organizations you do business with, as a company or as an individual. There is always one about which you say 'Never again!' and others where good service draws you back time after time, probably without your thinking that you have been sold to in a 'pushy' manner.

Promotion, selling and customer care act together to produce the right level of business. This is illustrated in Figure 8.1, as if the various influences are water flowing into a tank, with the outflow (sale) as the result.

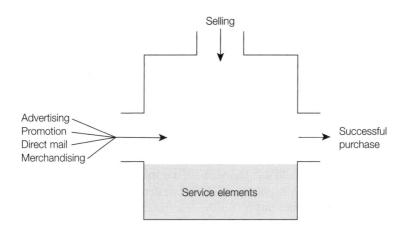

Figure 8.1 Sales are the net result of promotion, selling and
good service

BACKUP ACTIVITIES TO SUPPORT SALES AND SERVICE

Sales and service staff may succeed or fail largely through their
own personal approaches, but they are necessarily dependent on
the quality of the product or service that they sell, and the image
of the company for which they sell it. If any job is connected with
either quality or image, then it helps influence sales success.

This is more than simply saying that those on the production
line are involved. There are many more specific instances. Consider a few examples of people around an organization, who
might feel they have little or no relationship with 'marketing',
and how they influence things:

❏ someone in technical support handling a customer query not
only sorts out the problem, but also influences the likelihood
of the customer reordering;

❑ someone responsible for originating a computer system that ultimately interfaces with customers affects company image and thus the salesperson's relationship with customers;
❑ someone in accounts sorting out some complexity of VAT on a customer account affects the customer's image of the company for good or ill.

In some of these areas the normal expectation, and experience, of the customer is that any good impression of the company will be diluted. Who, on hearing the words 'It's in the computer', does not expect some inconvenience at his or her end? What are the equivalents of all this in your own organization?

The marketing-orientated organization loses no opportunity to maximize the impression given by both customer care and sales. They overlap, and both hold the possibility of assisting to make marketing better able to fulfil its intentions.

9

MANAGING THE CUSTOMER BASE

Customers vary, particularly in that some are larger than others. The concept of Pareto's Law, the so-called 80/20 rule, is important. This states that 20 per cent of customers will produce 80 per cent of the revenue and profit. The ratio will not, of course, be spot on, but it will probably be indicative. Different customers need different approaches. The power inherent in major customers easily makes the point. They can, to a degree, dictate terms, and the risk of losing them can make for an uneasy relationship.

DATABASE MARKETING

On the other hand, accelerated by recent developments in IT, marketing has come to have a focus closer and closer to the individual customer. Information can provide the basis for individual approaches, communication and management of customers in what is called 'database marketing'. Because of its growing importance, some of the principles involved are set out in this chapter. Whether used in a sophisticated or simple way these approaches can help make marketing more effective. Mass marketing activity continues to be important, but for many organizations – large and small – database marketing is now a key part of the mix.

Database marketing is any interactive and individual marketing, specifically promotion and communication activity, based on the use of information from a central database to direct its focus. In addition, it most often has a cycle of information inherent in its working: using information to direct an approach designed to prompt a response. This in turn provides new information, which can be returned to update the original database. The approaches used can include any of the many communications methods within the promotion mix.

Simplistically, database marketing is sometimes regarded as just 'sending out mailshots to customers and/or prospects'. But there is much more to it than that and, although direct mail is often involved, it should avoid the junk mail end of things. Rather it acts as a stimulus to ongoing and persuasive contact to build, maintain and develop customer relationships and, in so doing, it may use a full range of communications methods from telephone to newsletters, as well perhaps as direct mail. In addition, it may link to other personal contacts, for example the internal sales support office or the field sales force. Certainly it most often works in tandem with other marketing methods rather than being the sole way of relating to the market.

Figure 9.1 shows, in graphic form, an example of the kind of communications flow, and cycle of activity and events involved.

In looking at the chart, imagine a range of mixes. Some organizations use a predominantly database-orientated approach; others use it as part of a wider mix of methods. In either case the mix must be tailored to the particular product or service and the market in which it is sold in order to produce the best results.

It is characteristic of database marketing methodology – indeed it is one of its strengths – that it allows a considerable degree of both control and personalization. This applies, of course, to some contact methods more than others, for example a letter can be made individual and one to one, whereas public relations activity, a form of communication that may be an important part of the mix, is more general.

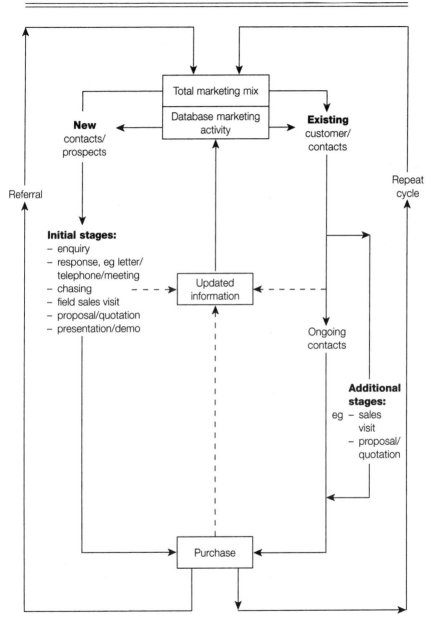

Figure 9.1 Database marketing

Creating a relationship

Perhaps the key to database marketing is in the word 'relation-ship'. By way of example, consider three letters from a typical morning's post. The first is from the bank, promoting pensions schemes for the umpteenth time. As the recipient has a good arrangement – and the bank should know this – yet another attempt to create interest is just an annoyance that does nothing to build the relationship. The second is from a motor distributor about a car supplied in the past. They do a good job of keeping in touch, one that is significant in influencing the view formed of their service. A telephone call to arrange for them to carry out the car's next service is willingly made. The third is a catalogue from a book club. This is less personally presented, but a past, perhaps regular, customer is probably happy to receive such a communication, and the chances are more business will transpire in the future.

The businesses in the above examples are all attempting, with varying degrees of effectiveness, to create and maintain customer relationships and to make them profitable. There is nothing new about that. What kick-started database marketing, making it into the thriving and growing area of methodology it now is, was the burgeoning development of computers. This, in turn, has made the management of the database itself easier and less costly, and has enabled accurate tailored approaches to be made to different groups of customers rather than a mass approach. Database marketing makes possible approaches that are more likely to find favour in the marketplace, because it allows action to be taken that more customers feel is well tailored to them as individuals.

THE KEY ADVANTAGES

The objectives for such approaches can be the same as for any other method of promoting goods and services, for example:

❑ to recruit new customers;
❑ to stimulate demand;
❑ to increase the frequency of purchase;
❑ to expand the take-up of the product range.

However, database marketing can have real, measurable advantages over other methods of promotion, as follows:

❑ *Selective*: Perhaps the greatest advantage is that of being able to focus communication on specific groups. It is what the distributor of a car does in sending material directed at an individual car owner, not as the purchaser of just a car, but of a particular model now so many years old. The distributor may even have variants of the approach for other customers, who have the same type of car but a different personal profile in terms of, say, age or home area.

❑ *Personal*: This goes closely with the above. It allows individual customers to be addressed by name – the distributor writes 'Dear Mr Brown' not 'Dear Motorist'. On other lists someone may be addressed as 'Dear Michael'. In each case the computer is set to prompt the appropriate form of address.

❑ *Measurable*: Because responses are, for the most part, linked specifically to individual action, it becomes possible to measure them, and thus the financial return that comes from them.

❑ *Adaptable*: Both the format and scale of approach can be tested and adapted to maximize returns. A communication can be sent to customers in one area of the country (or purchasers of just one product or any other limited category), for example, and results assessed before the approach is extended. Fine-tuning is also made possible along the way, with the nature and form of what is done evolving in the light of experience. The approach is adaptable too in terms of timing, and can be controlled so as to allow communications to go at exactly the right moment to coincide with the likelihood of a positive response (using knowledge of when that moment is).

THE LINK TO SERVICE

Such an individual approach coincides with what is happening in the market. In both industrial and consumer areas of marketing, the costs of mass marketing approaches are rising, and 'niche' marketing is focusing effort on smaller and smaller segments of groups of consumers, groups who value the individual approach, and are more likely to respond when treated as individuals. This aspect of database marketing makes it valuable in terms of competitiveness. There is a strong overlap with customer service. Dealing with customers in a way they find acceptable, and better still in a way they like and find more attractive than the way in which they are approached by others, builds loyalty and can increase sales at the expense of your competitors. Database marketing is important for its power to differentiate; and if marketing is about anything in competitive times, then it is certainly about differentiation.

All these factors make database marketing not so much a specialist technique as one that is available (and in many cases used) across a wide range of fields. Many readers will be familiar with it through approaches they receive from, for example: utilities, such as gas; telecommunications companies; banks, insurance companies and other financial services; charities; travel companies; retailers and mail order operations. All or part of those organizations' activities is database marketing. Larger organizations do not have a monopoly in their use of it, though some users certainly are large. Smaller organizations are also users and are doubtless intent on making their prospecting and contacts cost-effective. They do so by systematically communicating effectively with a smaller number of carefully selected people, rather than using a shotgun approach with many, possibly at greater cost and lesser return. The range of those using the technique means that, as with any technique, it is not necessarily universally well utilized, but it is certainly a proven methodology, which brings good results for many. Any approaches taken towards it must be thorough, and the first step is consideration of the basis for organization of the database itself.

DIVIDING THE MARKET

There is a dichotomy here. Groups intended for approach need to be large to produce economies of scale, or small if tailored approaches are to appeal to individuals. If database marketing is to work well in the market, then the smaller groups should predominate, and the computer system should enable this to be dealt with on a manageable and cost-effective basis.

In this form of segmentation (see Chapter 2), groupings must be established that are right for the individual business. This can involve demographics, the age, sex and other characteristics of those involved, or the size and type of companies. But it can also relate to many other possibilities of categorization, for example:

❑ customers and non-customers (or 'not-yet customers', as some say);
❑ large and small customers;
❑ recent, less recent and dormant customers;
❑ those relating to particular sources (responders to advertising or direct mail, or those with whom the sales team have had direct contact, for instance);
❑ purchasers of specific products;
❑ those in particular geographic areas, nationally or internationally;
❑ buyer types (in industry, ranging across directors, technical people and any particular level, job function or specialization that may be pertinent).

Other groups may occur to you that are more suited to your own business. For example, for some organizations intermediaries are important – an accountancy firm may obtain business by keeping in touch with banks. Groupings are not mutually exclusive; the most useful categories may be quite complex. A bookshop, for instance, might keep a list of those who have purchased a business book in the last year and live near enough to revisit the shop. (This is now duplicated by Internet book suppliers who send customers e-mail.) Categories may have greater complexity still.

With a computer system, summoning up the names of those meeting a number of specific criteria may take only a moment, though it is worth noting that, the more cross-referencing there is involved the longer it takes, and the more costly it is to keep records up to date.

The need for accuracy

The database must be accurate. This may sound obvious, but much of the information held on it can quickly date. Any information system must be capable of accurate and prompt update. Failure in this area means that not only does the system quickly become less cost-effective, with communications going to those who are off target, but also customer goodwill may rapidly dilute. Spelling a customer's name incorrectly may be forgiven as a one-off error, provided it does happen only once. Contacting a retired octogenarian about hang-gliding holidays three times in a week and addressing him as 'Dear Madam' destroys credibility and makes it very unlikely that he will plan any sort of holiday with the company.

DEVELOPING CONTACT STRATEGIES

Creating records may mean locating the names as well as entering them into the system or evolving less sophisticated customer and prospect records into a more usable form. Once records have been created, then a strategy needs to be adopted for their use. The possibilities are considerable, so the process is sensibly led by questions, for example:

❑ Are all target groups equally good prospects?
❑ What frequency of contact is appropriate for each group?
❑ What needs to be said to them?
❑ What method of communication (it may well be a mix) is to be used?
❑ What co-ordination, for example with the field sales force, is necessary?

The use of records must be actively planned. The longer-term sequence of contacts and the mix of methods are very important, as is the continuity. Consider the example of motor car suppliers. They have a number of opportunities. They want to service and if necessary repair cars. Ultimately they want to replace cars, and maybe sell others through the same customers (as someone might for a spouse or within a company). They may also seek the sale of extras and hope to prompt recommendations to others who might become new customers.

They should have information that categorizes each buyer, entered at first contact. They know something about the individuals, their organizations (if applicable) and motoring needs, and can plan the ongoing communication accordingly, aiming to create and build relationships, and instil trust and loyalty. This is a typical part of a sequence of contact, valid in many businesses, and planned to move people 'up the ladder' and through the stages necessary to create sales and revenue. It moves from suspects to prospects, to first-time buyers, to repeat customers, to regular customers, to major customers (buying across the range). Suppliers may also be aiming to influence advocates – those who recommend or influence others to buy. It is said that the first prerequisite to repeat business is to be remembered, which is sensible enough. However, any communication will quickly get boring if it only says: 'We're still here'.

Car distributors must create a sequence of sensible messages, for example:

❑ reminders of the next necessary service;
❑ an invitation to the launch of a new model;
❑ a note about some topical issue such as new legislation about tyre wear.

If personalizing the approach, adding an occasional incentive and ringing the changes in terms of contact method (eg alternating telephone and post) are well done, then it becomes very difficult for a customer – certainly one satisfied in the past – to take the car elsewhere.

However, none of this happens in a vacuum. Whatever communications are received, it is true that, as is said, 'loyalty is as good as the quality of the last supplier contact', and that quality is judged in the light of the impression created. This thread of communications also runs parallel with the actual process of doing business. Returning to the example of the car, if it is not serviced well or the personal courtesies are neglected, then the overall effect is destroyed or, at the very least, diluted. It is the systematic and creative use of the database as an integral part of the whole business that makes it an effective and differentiating process.

Information about contacts is used to decide the precise nature of the activity then deployed to communicate with them. If the information is right, if communications are helpful to customers (and prospects) in making decisions about what to do, if contacts seem up to date and accurate, and if approaches are seen as personal, individual and pertinent, then good results are likely to be produced. That is not to say this is a panacea for selling anything. The image, the product, the service – all the other factors inherent in marketing – retain their importance. Any technique is only as effective as the quality of the way it is implemented. The efficiency of the way in which contact is initiated, and the subsequent way in which customer relationships are nurtured, have a direct relationship to the level of business produced.

Attention to detail

In implementing these approaches, other factors need attention, for instance:

❑ Outgoing activity should be suitably coded, and steps taken to encourage feedback and ensure information is sought to verify the marketing method and update records.

❑ Such feedback can be summarized to produce overall information about trends, and provide assistance on a predictive basis as future activity is planned.

❑ The whole process can be linked back to such areas as marketing planning and product/service review, and act as a catalyst for change.

This integration of database activity with overall marketing and its direction extends its significance. Essentially, database activity is just one marketing method, which is instrumental in prompting sales of whatever is coming through at the moment. But by enhancing customer relationships, promoting feedback and acting to put the organization closer to the customer, it has broader implications. The information base can in various ways act as a corporate resource, for example contributing to the quality of business planning or product development. None of this is possible, however, without careful consideration of the systems aspects.

SYSTEM CONSIDERATIONS

The fast changing nature of anything and everything to do with technology is touched on in the next chapter. A few words are appropriate here, however, about the system on which the database is housed. Computer power is such that the hardware is less of a problem than it used to be (though sensible choices and possibly outside advice are necessary), but software certainly is. Specialist advice needs to be sought: options change as you watch and advice quickly dates. By 'specialist' is meant someone with an understanding of the application. There are, dare we suggest, some computer people with almost magical abilities, but who do not seem to live in the real world and would not recognize a customer if they fell over one.

Having said that the systems available change as you watch, there are perhaps three principal ways of progressing in this area. You can:

❑ bolt a marketing module on to an existing accounting package;
❑ purchase a package and fine-tune it to meet the specific needs involved;
❑ build your own database from scratch.

The first approach is likely to have drawbacks in that the original system was designed for rather different purposes. It may well make it difficult to include contacts or prospects in the way required in addition to the customers it is designed to deal with. The third approach is time-consuming, and often needs the kind of budget that dismays even the most adventurous. The package route makes good sense for most. The trick is to locate a basic package that is close to your requirements, so as to minimize the need for fine-tuning. Though some fine-tuning is likely to be necessary – after all, the whole purpose of the database is that it relates to specific marketing objectives – it is no place for too much compromise.

Note: Though it is beyond the limits of space to deal with the detail here, it should be noted that this area is covered (in the UK) by legislation. Anyone maintaining a database on computer must register with the Data Protection Registrar, and comply with regulations designed to prevent any threat to individuals by the misuse of databases. Details are available from The Office of the Data Protection Registrar, Springfield House, Water Lane, Wilmslow, Cheshire SK8 5AX.

THE INFORMATION NECESSITY

Every aspect of marketing must – above all – be customer-focused. The basis of marketing that incorporates the management of the customer record in this way is very simple. It is that marketing must utilize information to do a proper job, and that the best results do not come from seeing what information is available and using it in the best way possible, but from analysing what information is necessary to maximize the effectiveness of customer communication, assembling it and creating a system to make it conveniently usable. The right information and the right system, integrated into the total marketing process (and thus involving all the key members of the marketing team), can create genuine differentiation in the market and repay the initial cost and effort.

Knowing your customers and staying in contact with them are basic tenets of marketing. Approaches that are based on database marketing and initiate creative communications – providing real reasons to do business – can form a powerful element of many organizations' marketing activity. Database marketing needs careful application, and must be set up in such a way that it will enable cost-effective as well as persuasive contact to take place. It may just be an area that can make your marketing better.

10

THE ELECTRONIC REVOLUTION

This chapter is out of date. The pace of change means that by the time it has got into print, and you read it, things will have moved on. Having said that, it should not matter, at least within a reasonable time-frame, as what is most important is the trends and the attitude to information technology that must be taken with regard to marketing.

THE OFFICE ENVIRONMENT

The pace of change is frantic. Even considering the longer term, things move fast. Computers have revolutionized the office environment, but not everything has progressed as predicted. Consider the following:

❑ Computers themselves have perhaps evolved faster than initial predictions, but what has happened to the 'paperless office'? Most people's desks seem as submerged as ever (and some of it is computer printout).
❑ Computers make things more efficient and do things faster, but how long does it take to get to grips with the latest feature, and why have such phrases as 'Sorry, it's in the computer' become the ultimate excuse for delay?
❑ Computers have reduced costs, but what about the cost of equipment, training and peripherals?

These and no doubt other statements that could be made and questioned expose two sides of the proverbial coin. There is truth in both aspects of them. It is too simplistic to expect just to be able to say, 'Computers make things better', and expect there to be no downsides. The point about change remains. It took some years for computers to become established in every office, proportionately less for them to proliferate on to every desk, so that now most executives expect to type a good deal, perhaps all, of their written output. It took even less time from the introduction of e-mail to the point where people are not seen as serious players without it. New things may well consume us all even more quickly. We will see.

At the same time the pace of change does make problems. The cost of re-equipping or updating machinery, the training – formal or informal, it all takes time – and so on seem to continue endlessly. A new development may be real and useful, but it sometimes seems to last about five minutes. The little ditty below summarizes the feelings of many people as they are faced with the next new gizmo:

I bought a new computer
It came completely loaded
It was guaranteed for 90 days
But in 30 was outmoded.

Maybe such sentiments are only possible because of the computer industry's marketing success.

So far we have considered the area of office administration, but the electronic revolution has wide impact. Three areas deserve particular mention.

Products

The evidence for electronically influenced products is all around us. Some things are obviously electronic such as computers, computer games, digital cameras and personal organizers. Other things appear just electric, such as washing machines and fax machines, and there are yet others, such as cars. How many chips are there in all of these, and more? More products in the future will be in these general categories. Maybe some of them will be yours.

The whole process of product development in these circumstances becomes very different to the development of simpler things. Original development may:

❑ take longer;
❑ cost more;
❑ be more complex (and thus more likely to be problematical);
❑ be more vulnerable to competition.

We can all think of examples of the latter. Facsimile machines saw off telex in a moment. E-mail is replacing many fax messages (less special fax paper sold, and more normal paper as messages are printed out). Cassettes were largely sent on their way by compact discs, and a variety of music and video formats currently vie with each other to be the next 'standard'. This kind of dance is typical of many fields from software to toys; only the time-scale varies. Updating may follow very quickly. In some product areas new versions follow each other almost on a monthly basis.

Methodology

The way things work is being changed by technology. Right across the business world, the range of change is enormous. Think of the role that electronic money transfer and 'hole-in-the-wall' cash machines have had on bank branches; think too of the developing impact of Internet banking and where that may lead. Such things constitute big changes, and each example barely scratches the surface of what is going on.

Things change everywhere. Customers used to go into a shop, select goods, pay, and that was the end of it. Paying now involves electronic machines at the cash points. These do not just facilitate the taking of money (and make it possible to employ staff who cannot add up!); they are the tip of an electronic iceberg of integrated computer systems. The cash point registers the sale and communicates with stock control. More supplies of the product can be ordered automatically when stocks decline to a certain level. If a customer uses a card (increasingly, so-called 'smart' cards), whether a credit card or one linked to a loyalty scheme, then the sale can be recorded against that individual. If customers buy product X, they suddenly start receiving promotions through the post for product X or its competitors (supermarkets can charge their suppliers to send this sort of material on their behalf). Such schemes can be linked back to the cash point, so that offer coupons are distributed to particular customers in a way that reflects their buying record – or rather, in a way intended to influence their future buying.

Space prohibits a lengthy list of examples, but the current complexity and future possibilities are clear. There are certain matters that any particular organization must cope with. For example, a supermarket might be more resistant to seeing sales-people if their computer system is able to reorder directly. The salespeople then have to find new ways of prompting the discussions they want, which go a long way beyond reordering, and involve promotion, display and much else, and which are vital to the marketing effort.

As well as difficulties, there are also opportunities and areas where you can choose to get involved, despite greater complexity, if you see an advantage. For example, a search of what is new with an assessment of how it might help has become a prerequisite part of marketing thinking. Examples may well date, but the following show what is now possible, indeed what is now normal in terms of going about things:

❑ Computers can now calculate optimum merchandising arrangements. A company making a range of products different in size, price, margin and rate of turnover can work out, at the touch of a button, what mix of product selection should be put on any particular amount of shelving that a store allocates to their brand. No spare space is then left on the shelf and turnover and profit generation are maximized.

❑ Field sales staff now routinely carry computers and can use them to give an instant answer to customer questions about stock and delivery of a product.

❑ Customer details can be accessed instantly during transactions just by the mention of, say, a postcode; this facilitates many processes, for example dealing at a distance from a call centre.

Computer and other IT developments will doubtless produce many more changes of this sort. These changes will either actively assisting marketing effort, or marketing will have to fit in with them if it is to retain credibility.

Electronic marketing

The other major area, and one subject to continuing change and development, is that of the Internet and e-commerce. These tend to be spoken of as if they are something new. In fact, though *how* they operate is clearly new, the effect they have is to add to the choice of methodology available in two different areas: promotion and distribution. Let us take these in turn.

Promotion

Web sites, for all their technical wizardry, are only another method of communicating with customers (and sometimes – see 'Distribution' below – of doing business). Consider the Web site, first and foremost, as a promotional channel. As such it must command attention, put over its message clearly and act to persuade. It must also be convenient and easy to use. (See box 'Help, please'.) The Web site may be an electronic alternative to many things: a brochure, a salesperson, a showroom or shop window, a magazine or more (in any combination).

Distribution

This is the territory of e-commerce. The whole business transaction, or most of it, takes place over the airwaves, so to speak. The point about clarity and convenience made above is perhaps even more important here. Some things are up and running and working well. Customers may conduct their banking and finances through Internet accounts; they may order many things – computers, pizzas, books, CDs, etc – from Internet sites. One point about this that will be worth watching is the relationship between Internet shopping and conventional retailing.

Some things can work fine exclusively through Internet channels. If people want to buy a new novel by a favourite author, they are probably happy not even to look at it – they tap into Amazon.com or whoever, call up the title and place their order (with maybe a little price comparison along the way). Other purchases are more complex. If someone wants a new CD player, say, they may well want to look at it – better still hear it and check it out. They go to a retailer and do just that. Then they might elect to visit a number of sites on the Internet, compare prices, check delivery and so on, and place an order. What many people will not do is simply order a machine seen only on a monitor screen.

In other words retailing is currently necessary for certain kinds of e-commerce to work. What future buying practice will be like is still uncertain. That said, e-commerce works well for many things, the fields in which it operates are growing, and more and more people are either experimenting with this sort of shopping or expressing confidence in it and becoming regulars. Current predictions for the farther future include the demise of super-markets. All bulk goods, from tissues to cat food, will be ordered over the Internet and delivered. Customers will only visit stores for things that demand real choice or checking; as a result, stores will be smaller, but departments such as the bakery or cheese counter will expand. Again we will see.

HELP, PLEASE

An important fact about the nature of Web sites is worth emphasizing. They must be customer-focused. This may seem obvious, but it also means that they should *not* necessarily:

❑ incorporate everything that is technologically possible (perhaps just because someone regards doing so as a challenge);

❑ be comprehensive (some things that might be incorporated are surely more important than others);

❑ be interactive in every possible way (though there may be strong reasons for having an interactive element);

❑ incorporate every technological gizmo known (some sites will aim for customers who are more technically sophisticated or demanding, but it should be recognized that not everyone is of this persuasion – at least not yet).

The objectives that give a Web site its *raison d'être* should be customer-orientated – it should be designed to work in the way they want, or at least like, and to do so without any great gaps in its capability.

An example will illustrate the point. One evening, one of the authors of this book contacted two Web sites. One was Amazon.com, the US bookseller (they sell more than books, but it was a book order that prompted the contact). The site is especially clear and easy to use. All was going well, a few interesting minutes were spent checking out soon-to-be-published books in favourite areas and an order was placed. Then a problem materialized (about credit cards – the details do not matter). The system did not cope with this, and the user's understanding did not cope with how to deal with it either. In a shop, of course, you would just ask, and it was the same here – a message was sent by e-mail, and a prompt reply spelt out clearly exactly what needed to be done. No problem. When a site works this well people will return (even those who do not see themselves as being at the forefront of things electronic).

The same evening another site was contacted. It was a nightmare of insufficient information and confusion (it would be unkind to name it) and after some minutes of struggle, frustration and travelling in electronic circles, any attempt to do business with it was abandoned.

The difference was very obvious, and yet why should one be so good and the other so poor? After all the technology is there. Some sites work and get customers saying 'This is good' whatever the technical sophistication of the site. A simple one is certainly able do a good job and make customers feel it is good. The difference is probably in the approach. Maybe the second site had been set up too quickly. Maybe it had been created on the assumption that customers are clairvoyant or maybe the objectives for the site were unclear.

Whatever the reason, the point here is clear. Do business in this way and you expose yourself – no order materialized in this example. Assuming they contact you at all, people will notice how your site works (not least compared with others sites), they will talk about it to others and they will elect to come back – or not. Image is affected; so are future business prospects. Going about the set-up process needs care and consideration, and it to this that we turn next.

GOING ELECTRONIC

A complete rundown on the methods of marketing incorporating the Internet is beyond our brief here. However, some guidelines about the set-up and role of a Web site follow (drawing on the section 'Web sites' in Chapter 6), both as practical advice in their own right, and as examples of the thinking and approaches that need to be applied in this area.

The job of setting up a Web site can be time-consuming and expensive, and so too can be the job of maintaining it and keeping it up to date. Some organizations acted very early as technology created this opportunity, though some acted solely because it was flavour of the month, 'something that had to be done', perhaps to keep up with others, perhaps to pander to the ego of someone involved and enthusiastic. Whatever the reasons, there are certainly examples where such early action was ill considered (or indeed not considered), and where time and money were spent to no good effect. Such an initiative needs thinking through; the first question is very obvious and straightforward.

What are the objectives that you have for your Web site?

It is not suggested that there will be only one. Several are likely, but they should all be spelt out and be specific. Ultimately it will be important to know whether the cost of set-up is delivering what was intended, and this is important to how a site is developed. Two particular purposes predominate:

1. *A reference point*: Perhaps the site is in part a source of reference. You want people to consult it to obtain information (and be impressed by it at the same time). For example, many accountants have sites on which you can check current tax information or rates. This sort of site may save time and effort that would otherwise be expended in other ways. Perhaps you intend a site to play a more integral part in the overall sales and marketing process. In that case, you want to measure its effectiveness in terms of counting the number of new contacts it produces and, in turn, how many of those are, in due course, turned into actual paying customers.
   Note: If you already have a Web site, check whether you have good feedback on its use and the specific results it brings you (for example, counting new contacts or revenue coming from new contacts). Similarly if you are in the process of setting up a site, ensure that consideration of feedback information is an inherent part of the process.
2. *An ordering point*: In addition, you may have products you want people to order and pay for through direct contact with the site. For example, consultants might offer a survey of some sort, primarily to put an example of their expertise and style in the hands of prospective clients (though it might also be a source of revenue). A product company might, of course, have their whole range listed and available to order from the site. In this case, not only must the ordering system work well, and this means it must be quick and easy for whoever is doing the ordering, but the follow-up must be good, too. Any initial good impression given will quickly evaporate if whatever is ordered takes for ever to arrive or needs several chasers. One hazard

to good service is to demand too much information as an order is placed. Some facts are key and, of course, this kind of contact represents an opportunity to create a useful database; but turning ordering into an experience reminiscent of the Spanish Inquisition will hardly endear you to people.

Three distinct tasks

With clear objectives set, there are then three distinct tasks that must be fulfilled. They are to:

1. *Attract people to the site*: Just having the site set up does not mean people will log on to it in droves, much less that the specific type of people you want to do so will act in this way. Other aspects of wider promotion must draw attention to it and this may vary from simply having the Web site address on your letterhead to incorporating mention (and perhaps demonstration) of it into a range of promotional methods from advertisements to brochures. Simple, cost-effective methodology may work well here with just a promotional postcard acting to prompt people (customers or others) to investigate the site.
2. *Impress people when they see it*: This applies to both its content and its presentation. It means keeping a close eye on the customers' view and accommodating all the necessary practicalities as it is set up. For example, all sorts of impressive graphics are possible, can look creative and may well inform and impress. Certainly you will need some. But such devices take a long time to download, and if that is what you are encouraging people to do, they may find it tedious (at worst curtailing their contact because of its time-consuming nature). This is more likely if the graphics seem more like window-dressing than something that enhances the content in a genuinely useful way.
3. *Encourage repeat use*: This may or may not be one of the objectives. If it is, then efforts have to be made to encourage re-contacting (again using a whole range of prompts) and this

too may involve an overlap with other forms of communication.

In addition to the points made above, you will also need to
consider carefully:

❑ *site content*: what should be presented (this is an ongoing job,
not a one-off);
❑ *interaction*: how the contacting of the Web site can prompt a
dialogue;
❑ *topicality*: how up to date it should be (this affects how regularly
it needs revision, from daily to annually);
❑ *ease of use*: its convenience and accessibility (does it have a
suitable navigation mechanism?);
❑ *image*: whether it will look consistent (and not as if it has been
put together by committee);
❑ *security*: the protection it needs (is anything confidential, is it
vulnerable to hackers and will customers feel their own information is safe?).

Overall, it will need the same planning, co-ordination and careful
execution as any other form of marketing communication. In
addition, it is likely to necessitate active, ongoing co-operation
from numbers of people around the organization who will provide
and update information. This may be a larger job than it appears
at first sight, not just because of the numbers of individuals and
departments involved, but because they may have differing
perspectives (with, say, research and marketing differing in the
depth of technical information that should be included).

This aspect can present quite a challenge, especially in an
organization of any size. Clearly, responsibility for the site and
what it contains must be laid unequivocally at someone's door,
together with the appropriate authority to see it through. Another
challenge may be to get computer and marketing people to work
effectively together. Marketing must, for instance, ensure that
computer staff understand the objectives and do not proceed on
the basis of including everything that is technically possible (or,
at the risk of upsetting computer experts, that is just fun to do).

At the same time, someone needs to have the knowledge that is necessary from a technical standpoint. This may be internal or external, but it needs to be linked to an understanding of marketing and/or the ability to accept a clear brief if an appropriate scheme is to be created. There is a real danger of simply applying all the available technology, building in every bell and whistle simply because it is possible. Practical solutions are necessary to meet clear objectives (and these should always be customer-focused).

If a site is to be useful, that is, an effective part of the marketing mix, then sufficient time and effort must be put in to get it right. The ongoing job of maintaining it must be borne in mind from the beginning.

Additional possibilities

Linking in research

An interesting and practical development is the availability of standard, cost-effective software packages that can work as an integral part of a Web site and monitor how it is used. In fact, there are now such add-ons that are better described as 'research tools'. One such, ONQUEST, not only allows regular research and formal monthly analysis about exactly who is using a Web site, their precise characteristics, and how and why they are in touch with the site, but also allows the way the system works to be tailored simply to the needs and intentions of an individual user. The intention is specifically to obtain information that will make the Web site a more accurate and effective marketing tool. (Details of the ONQUEST system can be obtained from Strategy, Research & Action Ltd (tel 0181 878 9482). Their managing director, Robin Birn, the researcher who instigated this particular version of the technique, has written about it in *Effective Use of Market Research* (1999), published by Kogan Page.)

Linking to sales

Similarly there are now systems that allow visitors to a Web site to click in a way that institutes their receiving a telephone call to discuss some specific detail of an offer. This can be instant and online, so that both parties can look at the site on screen and discuss it. Alternatively a call can be made a few minutes later. It depends on the system. Such a contact is, of course, essentially a sales one. If it is made sufficiently easy, then it will generate conversations that influence the likelihood of sales and which might otherwise never have occurred.

Utilizing appropriate technology

Some applications are particularly well suited to a specific product or service. For example, it is possible to book a hotel following a detailed inspection of it over the airwaves. Before long, customers will do this in a way that is almost as real as walking around the actual building. It parallels what many customers want to do. If a real alternative to visiting a hotel is provided, something that is judged by its users as better than any sort of brochure, then a particular provider will have an edge in the market against competitors.

It is said that the future is not what it used to be. Certainly marketing people have a whole new area of activity, and new skills as well, to get to grips with. Precisely how it can – and will – affect you over the next months and years may be uncertain. That it *will* affect you is not.

One sure way of being better at marketing in the future is to get to grips with what needs to be done in this area. It needs careful consideration (it is not something to jump at) and whatever is done will need care in implementation. It is not something that can ever be got 'right', and put on one side as needing no more care and attention. For better or for worse we are all faced with an ongoing process as change continues and new elements of it come into view. It presents both a challenge and an opportunity, and marketing is inherently about the creative exploitation of opportunities.

11

CO-ORDINATION, CONTROL AND CULTURE

This is intentionally a short chapter, not because the factors referred to in it are unimportant (they are crucial), but because the detail, and implementation, of what is involved must be specific to each individual organization. A number of matters are, however, worth brief comment.

ORGANIZING THE MARKETING FUNCTION

In order to achieve objectives, some form of planning system is needed. This, in turn, demands an organization structure both to create marketing plans and to implement them. Being a *marketing* organization (ie consumer-orientated), the structure should be built from the bottom up. This process starts by identifying what services consumers desire from the company, and what activities must be in train in order to persuade people to buy. This will help specify the nature and scale of, for example, the sales effort required. Likewise, the management structure relating to field sales can be identified by asking what support salespeople need in terms of its nature and scale in order that their activities are effective and well controlled.

Overall, whatever the form of marketing organization adopted, care must be given to its integration with other functions of the company.

Control in marketing is conceptually similar to other forms of management control. It depends upon the comparison of Actual performance against pre-set Standards and the taking of corrective action based upon the resulting Variances:

$A - S = V$

The objectives and plans will dictate the basis of the standards. Thus, the sales plan will contain sales forecasts, which can be translated into targets for each salesperson.

Many of the promotion areas have been traditionally viewed as immeasurable. Undoubtedly it is difficult to assess and control activities that depend, for the most part, upon human reaction and cannot be easily separated from other influences. The difficulty has been exacerbated, however, by attempting to evaluate each part in terms of the whole. Thus, 'How much will advertising affect sales?' is usually an unanswerable question, as sales do not depend upon advertising alone.

If, however, it is clearly specified what the advertising is supposed to do, ie impress a certain message on a certain number of people of a certain type, then it is feasible to define standards of performance and evaluate its achievement.

Control of a different kind can and should be exercised in marketing. All marketing activities are quantifiable in financial terms, and therefore budgetary control can be exercised. For marketing activities to be effective, it is not enough that each department should be well run. The whole marketing function needs to be integrated and well co-ordinated with the rest of the company.

IMPLEMENTING AND CONTROLLING THE PLAN

A marketing plan, deriving from a SWOT analysis and the other processes referred to earlier (see Chapter 2), should spell out three key elements of the activity that it plans. These are:

❑ objectives;
❑ strategies;
❑ tactics.

These are illustrated in Table 11.1.

Table 11.1 Planning elements

Concepts	Illustrations	Contents
Objectives	The corporate destination	What needs to be achieved. This must be expressed by objectives that are: S Specific M Measurable A Achievable R Realistic T Timed
Strategies	The *road* the company will travel to reach its destination	A description of how the company will achieve its objectives: S Segments A Audience P Product features/benefits
Tactics	The *vehicle* used to carry the company along its strategic road	A description of: P People responsible A Actions to be completed M Methods to be employed

Successful implementation depends upon the effective management of five resources:

1. *what*: the goals, objectives, aims;
2. *who*: the people responsible or accountable for plan realization;
3. *where*: the specific, identified, quantified marketplaces;
4. *when*: the period covered by the plan;
5. *why*: the reasons, desired outcomes.

It will perhaps be the marketing manager's responsibility to ensure that all material marketing resources are in place. These could well include:

❑ product;
❑ packaging;
❑ internal promotion aids (sales aids);
❑ external promotion campaigns (eg advertising);
❑ budgetary management systems;
❑ sales data systems;
❑ performance standards.

Once the plan is launched, the emphasis of attention changes to control. The plan should contain specific financial, marketing, sales, distribution and promotion objectives. These provide a basis for performance standards in a number of key areas, including product sales (in value terms), product sales (in volume terms) and product sales (in market share terms, if appropriate).

Performance standards can be expressed as follows:

❑ *Annual targets*: These express performance expectations in sales, profit and market-share terms. Annual targets are known as absolute targets. Variances from these targets will identify what has gone right or wrong, but not *why*.
❑ *Moving standards*: These express the annual targets in moving divisions of the plan period, ie monthly or quarterly actual figures, cumulative figures and trends. Although moving standards can forecast deviations from plan, they will not identify *why* performance is greater or less than the required targets.
❑ *Diagnostic standards*: These *can* identify what is causing the variations and why, and may indicate an appropriate action.

Table 11.2 amplifies these points.

Type of control	Objective of control	Standards	How to measure performance	Examples of what to look for
1. Annual product plan control	To examine if plan objectives are being achieved	Sales quotas and market-share financial targets	Comparison of actual results against standards set in each area of performance	Notable shortfall between standard and actual; failure of individual sales territories to achieve sales targets by buyer category
2. Profitability control	To examine if financial objectives are being met	Profitability by product or product group	Comparison of actual results against standards	Major shift in production mix; spending levels above plan levels; declining sales
3. Efficiency/ productivity control	To evaluate and improve results of marketing expenditures	Promotional deadlines Distribution targets Sales force activities	Comparison of actual results against advertising plan; sales force: who called on/how many/call frequency/ what done in each call	Failure to meet deadlines or set standards in each area of promotion

Table 11.2 Marketing plan control

VARIANCE ANALYSIS

Variances are calculated by comparing actual results against the pre-set standards.

First, use cumulative totals so that individual monthly variations will tend to cancel each other out.

Second, use moving annual totals (MATs) by taking 12 months' performance up to and including the month in question. As each month is added and the same month of the previous year is deducted, the trend in the moving annual total will indicate present performance compared with the same period in the previous year.

This enables comparisons to be made on a single diagram of monthly performance against target, cumulative performance against target and, via the moving annual total, the present year versus the previous year. The benefit of a good control system and feedback mechanism is that it enables managers quickly to identify s*ales performance variances and the true reasons for them, and to react to changed circumstances.* By controlling the plan they will be in a position to report monthly, and answer the following questions that may be raised by top management:

❑ Are the plan objectives being met?
❑ What are the variances between budget and actual?
❑ What are the causes of these variances?
❑ What actions are being taken to correct them?
❑ Is a re-forecast or re-budget necessary?

Marketing activity cannot guarantee success but, carefully applied, it will certainly increase the likelihood.

Note: in a commercial environment, an organization's success is measured by its profitability. For those interested in how this is defined, the text below sets out further detail.

The profit mechanism

The best overall measurement of corporate performance is usually taken to be return on capital employed (R/CE). This ratio is calculated by expressing net profit (usually before tax) (R) as a percentage of capital employed (CE). Capital employed is calculated by taking the total assets less the current liabilities, which is equivalent to the fixed liabilities, the long-term money. (These terms are explained below.)

GUIDE TO 10 KEY FINANCIAL TERMS

1. *Return*: Net profit (usually before tax and sometimes before interest charges where levied by a parent company on a subsidiary).
2. *Capital employed*: Fixed assets plus working capital.
3. *Fixed assets*: Money tied up in land, buildings, plant and machinery.
4. *Current assets*: Money tied up in stock, work in progress, debtors, cash, etc.
5. *Current liabilities*: Money owed in the short term, eg creditors, overdraft, tax, dividends.
6. *Working capital*: Current assets minus current liabilities.
7. *Fixed liabilities*: The long-term money in the company, ie shareholder's equity, long-term loans, retained profits.
8. *Margin*: Sales revenue minus cost of goods sold.
9. *Balance sheet*: The overall statement of a company's position at one moment in time, usually at the end of the financial year, showing the sources of the money in the company (fixed liabilities and current liabilities) and how it is deployed (fixed assets and current assets).
10. *Profit and loss account*: A statement showing the results of a company's trading in the period, indicating revenue, expenditure and thus profit.

The primary ratio of R/CE is a function of two secondary ratios: return (R) on sales (S) multiplied by turnover of the capital employed (the latter ratio being the number of times the capital employed is utilized in generating sales revenue). The basic profit mechanism of the company can be represented thus:

$$\frac{R}{CE} = \frac{R}{S} \times \frac{S}{CE}$$

This equation, in turn, depends upon other ratios. A change in return on sales must be due to a movement in one or any combination of the following four factors: sales volume; price; cost; product mix.

A potentially dangerous future position can easily be masked if figures such as sales volume and revenue are viewed in isolation. If volume increases have been achieved by price-cutting, or revenue expanded by, say, selling more of a range of low-margin products, then ratio analysis will help identify the concomitant risk to profitability.

A change in capital turnover will be caused by either a rise or fall in the utilization of fixed assets and/or of working capital. Furthermore, if the turnover of working capital has altered, then it must be as a result of relative change in the relationships of current assets and/or current liabilities to sales. Analysis of capital utilization in this way can help reveal that an apparently successful sales campaign has created such a build-up in debtors that profitability has suffered.

By this process of reasoning a ratio hierarchy can be developed down to departmental level, which will analyse total company operations. Figure 11.1 shows a typical ratio chart.

IDENTIFYING THE PROFIT INPUT OF MARKETING

A ratio tree covers total company operations, and can be used to identify marketing's contribution to profit-making. Most sales and marketing people will recognize their responsibilities in the R/S portion of the equation; this is a natural development from the sales-oriented approach. In this half of the hierarchy, the ratios can be employed very effectively to analyse the reasons for

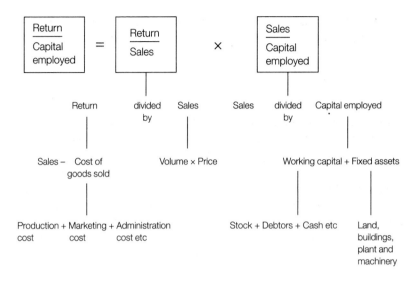

Figure 11.1 Typical ratio chart

performance change. It is usually illuminating to identify the relative importance of volume, price, cost and mix changes, particularly in those companies that seem to believe the solution to every profitability problem is to increase sales volume.

There are some problems. For example, it is easy for sales management to fail to recognize their input into the S/CE part of the mechanism. As Figure 11.1 shows, two of the major components of working capital are stocks and debtors. Although sales managers may not directly control credit granting, debt collection and stock availability, their policies must have an impact on them and thus on the profitability of the company. Interestingly there is a paradox here. If sales managers wish to increase their sales volume, two of the tactics they might well use are immediate ex-stock delivery and generous credit terms. Whilst such inducements to customers will almost certainly increase sales and probably the R/S half of the equation, they could have a disastrous effect on the sales/capital employed area, leading ultimately to lower profitability in terms of the ratio R/CE.

This quick analysis of the marketing input to the profit mechanism immediately shows up areas of responsibility that need to be defined:

❑ Who should set stock levels?
❑ Who should control credit when it is used as a promotional tool?
❑ Is the product mix sufficiently specified and controlled?

It should be possible in every company to identify which managers are to be responsible for which ratios. That alone is a major step forward in planning and controlling the business effectively, if only because it highlights any inter-functional conflicts that must be resolved. For example, if production managers are wholly responsible for finished stock levels they will tend to keep them low to save cost. Sales managers given that authority may well decide to increase both the range and the depth of the stocks in order to capitalize on every sales opportunity. Usually some compromise must be reached in the light of the impact on overall profitability.

THE PEOPLE ELEMENT

All the above has been concerned with the numbers. Make no mistake, the numbers are important. In commercial organizations, profit is the driving force. It not only pays the salaries and wages, but it also provides a return for the shareholders, and the wherewithal (which may, of course, be augmented by borrowing) to finance future growth through investment. But business, and therefore marketing, is about people. Take the people out of any business and you are left with very little, and certainly with very little that is going to do anything of its own volition.

The range of people in marketing is considerable, from sales executives calling on customers on the other side of the world to computer experts designing marketing control systems and advertising people dreaming up the next creative idea that will make future advertising work effectively. All need their own talents and skills, though all must share a common customer orientation.

What about marketing directors? (And director is right, because marketing is, or should be, a top management function.) Who is likely to do this job, and what kind of person is likely to do it best? Classic marketing people have probably come up the organizational ladder through one of the principal tactical task areas – research, product development, pricing, or distribution – or the communication areas – public relations, advertising and/ or promotion, or selling. They must know something of them all. The priorities vary, but some are universal. All marketing people need to be persuasive communicators, and most will have had some direct customer contact. While it is impossible for them to be able to do everything, they must be expert in key areas. They must be good managers. Usually numbers of people are involved in the marketing process, and they must be found, developed and a plan and organization worked out for them. They must be controlled and motivated; and all this and more takes up just as much time, and demands just as much skill, as that required of any manager leading a group of people and responsible for achieving results *through* them.

But marketing also needs direction. Those who wear the marketing hat have to be able to see the broad view, the long term. They must be strategists, not only with vision, but able to put together all the elements necessary to implement a marketing plan that sets out *how* to achieve chosen objectives; and they must do so in a way that recognizes other functions within the company and works constructively with them.

Better marketing demands more. There is a need for numeracy, decision-making and various interactive skills: negotiation, presentational ability and communications are vital. (Marketing people may only reach the appropriate standard in many of these through training – they are not born able to do this range of things, though they may well have inherent creativity.) They must work systematically, spotting opportunities, collecting and analysing information, and taking and seeing through action that will achieve their aims, yet balance all this with the other intentions of the organization and others in it. It is no easy task; and in a company of any size several – often many – people are involved. It is a team effort, and the net result must be to seek success creatively in the marketplace and do so on a continuous basis.

None of this can happen in isolation. Those in marketing must interact effectively with many other people and departments around the company. Some it leads, and some it is supported by, but all are needed. Marketing must recognize this. It has a responsibility to inform others of these links because, if they work well, they make it more likely that the company will thrive and meet its objectives in the marketplace. There is a strong case for saying that every organization will do better if it has a marketing culture; this is a theme that is picked up in the Afterword, and it provides an appropriate point at which to end this review.

SUMMARY

Remember the four questions posed in Chapter 3 in discussing planning:

1. Where are we now?
2. Where do we want to go?
3. How will we get there?
4. How will we know when we get there?

In simple terms, control answers the final question. It not only answers it, but allows opportunity for fine-tuning of performance, a hand on the tiller to adjust course when things are not going exactly to plan and, just as important, the possibility of taking advantage of changes that present (sometimes unexpected) opportunities. With this in mind, we see how important co-ordination is to the marketing process. The progression from planning to implementation to control in a continuing cycle (illustrated in Figure 11.2) is as important overall as any of the individual elements; together they make the process work.

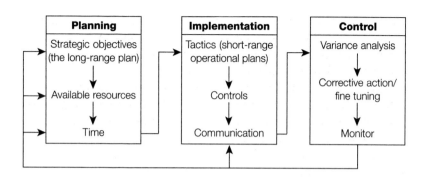

Figure 11.2 Implementing and controlling the marketing plan

With all of this, good factual information is the basis of the best decisions, and any source of good information is to be welcomed. Marketing can only be effective based on hard fact. One way of making it better may be to tighten things up in this area.

AFTERWORD

A final word that takes us back from dissection to marketing in the round concludes this review. As we have seen, being better at marketing is, in part, in the details of execution: selecting what to do, doing so creatively and making implementation effective. There are larger issues, however, and the approaches adopted to these are also important.

The first issue is undoubtedly *customer focus*. Every aspect of marketing activity must be based on an understanding of customers. Taking the customers' views into account is the basis for any sort of marketing success, and not doing so the most likely reason for failure. From planning to execution, this principle must be at the forefront of your mind if you are to make marketing work effectively.

Secondly, marketing must be *sustained continuously*. In any business, particularly the smaller one, it is easy to be distracted. There are so many tasks – and problems – concerned with running a business, and these can result in time being taken away from attention to marketing. Either time is reduced, or it ends up being applied *ad hoc*, when other pressures permit – or both. But customers need continuous communication, and service; they need constant reminder. If you are not in touch, you can be sure that someone else is. This applies to everything from individual sales effort to something like advertising. Timing is dictated by customers and their perspective, and must not be dictated by what is internally convenient. Attention here can result directly in better marketing.

Thirdly, the various disparate activities of marketing must be *co-ordinated*. Unless things are set up to interrelate and act together, then the impact they have will be diluted. Such co-ordination starts with planning, and can involve punctilious project management, but is well worth while. Any failure here – advertising breaking ahead of the product being available, for example – dilutes effectiveness and, at worst, can sabotage the results targeted. Similarly, when one activity builds on another, and the timing and relationships between activities are well judged, then marketing effectiveness strengthens and results are likely to be improved.

Fourthly, marketing is, as has been said, as much an art as a science. That is not to devalue those aspects that are more scientific or quantifiable, but rather to emphasize the need for a *creative approach*. It is the new ideas and approaches that can differentiate, and lift routine, competent marketing activity to the level of something special. If this implies taking certain risks, so be it. That goes with the territory. Anything that directs us elsewhere is to be avoided. Nothing should be done solely because that was the way it was done in the past. Repeat the effective things by all means, but make sure they are constantly reviewed, invigorated by new ideas or changed in the light of new circumstances. Ideas come in all shapes and sizes. The trick is not to search for a revolutionary idea that transforms everything (though it is good if you find some). It is more to approach every detail of marketing activity in a spirit of creativity, and constantly fine-tune the methodology in a way that constantly keeps marketing activity fresh and helps it better meet its goals.

A final thought: marketing is too important to be thought the exclusive province of marketing people, or the marketing department. It involves people very widely across an organization. If people do not understand marketing, or their role within it, that is down to the marketing people. It is their task to *create a marketing culture*, so that such understanding exists, and indeed so that it prompts action on an ongoing basis, leading to everything and everybody within an organization supporting the marketing activity on which their success, and that of the organization as a whole, ultimately rests.

No one should believe marketing is easy, but it is necessary and it is possible. Many of the things that need to be done are, at root, based on common-sense approaches. Of course there is skill in all the techniques and approaches that are involved, and of course – given the unsympathetic and competitive outside world – success is not a foregone conclusion. But marketing, good and effective marketing, makes the difference. When it does work, it is rarely a question of 'good luck' – there are almost always people who can look back with satisfaction because their active approach has created the success achieved.

It is a process that never stops. The most successful marketing activity must always be made better to create a way of working that works as well in the future as it has in the past.

REFERENCES

Birn, R J (1999) *Effective Use of Market Research*, Kogan Page, London

Forsyth, P (1996) *101 Ways to Increase Sales*, Kogan Page, London

Forsyth, P (1997) *How to be Better at Writing Reports and Proposals*, Kogan Page, London

Forsyth, P (1999) *Everything You Need to Know about Marketing*, Kogan Page, London

Forsyth, P (2000) *Marketing on a Tight Budget*, Kogan Page, London

INDEX